# ACADEMIC HORIZONS

Hye-Jin Hawkes
Michael Brandon
Hugh Newton
Kimberley Blount

## Skills Across Disciplines

**ACADEMIC HORIZONS**: Skills Across Disciplines
College English Education Committee (CEEC), Hanyang University
—
Writers: Hye-Jin Hawkes, Michael William Brandon, Hugh Newton and Kimberley Blount
Editors: Yuah V. Chon, Kyungsook Kim and Hye-Jin Hawkes
Reviewers: Yuah V. Chon, Kyungsook Kim, Hye-Jin Hawkes and Connie Park
—

—
Published by HANYANG UNIVERSITY PRESS
Tel. 02.2220.1432-4
Web. http://press.hanyang.ac.kr
Email. presshy@hanyang.ac.kr
—
ISBN 978-89-7218-799-8 (93740)

# ACADEMIC HORIZONS

Basic Liberal Arts Courses of

## Skills Across Disciplines

HANYANG UNIVERSITY

한양대학교 대학영어교육위원회 편

Hye-Jin Hawkes
Michael Brandon
Hugh Newton
Kimberley Blount

한양대학교 출판부

# Foreword

This book has been developed to help students on their pathway to academic success. Academic skills, often overlooked in university programs, are crucial, and this book is designed to provide students with a guide to approaching academic assignments. It covers all aspects from the initial research planning phase to the professional skills required for presenting, along with the application of these skills in academic writing.

Sharing their knowledge of academic research, conference presentations, and published writing, the writers and editors have compiled this book to guide you toward greater academic achievement. The skills and insights offered are authentic, and we are confident that they will better prepare you for the demands of your academic and professional work.

# How to Use this Book

At the beginning of any academic journey lies the planning phase. Whether preparing a short written assignment or a large research project, it is important to gather your ideas. This includes understanding existing ideas in the field and identifying your distinct area of focus. The first chapter of this book, **Research and Information Gathering**, will guide you through these initial steps, and allow you to be fully prepared for your assignment or project. A strong project requires not only original thought, but also solid data support. This chapter will equip you to do just that.

The second chapter, **Writing**, takes you through the process of developing an academic paper. Covering aspects from structural elements to integrating evidence and citation, this chapter provides all the fundamental information necessary to successfully translate your ideas into written form. It also details how academic language differs from other writing styles, with Sections 4. Coherence and 5. Academic Language focusing on essential elements of academic writing.

Academic research is not just about writing; it also involves presenting your ideas to an audience. The third chapter, **Academic Presentation** explores ways to bring your presentation to life. It covers the basics of presentation structure, skills for effective delivery, and designing visual aids to support your presentation and engage the audience.

Structured to allow you to either dive into specific sections or follow step-by-step, this book serves as a comprehensive guide. Each section draws on the writers' experiences, ensuring you gain skills applicable in both academic and professional settings. Allow this book to broaden **your** academic horizons.

College English Education Committee (CEEC) **Textbook Team**

## Acknowledgement

This textbook development was supported and funded by the College English Education Committee (CEEC), Center for Creative Convergence Education at Hanyang University. We extend our gratitude for their ongoing support throughout the project.

This book, ***Academic Horizons: Skills Across Disciplines*** would not have been possible without the dedicated and ongoing collaborative efforts of the textbook team members. They all shared their professional knowledge, teaching experience and teaching philosophy to produce the most relevant, up-to-date and easy-to-learn textbook for undergraduate students from a variety of language backgrounds. Their best interest in developing this textbook was to provide standardized professional academic skills materials but at the same time a customized book especially for university students in Hanyang University.

First of all, we would like to give thanks to the writers, Michael Brandon, Hugh Newton, Hye-Jin Hawkes and Kimberley Blount for their dedication to writing Academic Horizons: Skills Across

Disciplines for the last 12 months in the middle of their busy schedules. Michael Brandon wrote Chapter 3, and contributing professional knowledge to it with extensive research and experience presenting at a range of international conferences. Hugh Newton and Hye-Jin Hawkes wrote Chapters 1 and 2. Hugh Newton, who has experience in writing several books of creative writing, shared his expertise in developing content in the writing section. Hye-Jin Hawkes, writer and editor in this project, has experiences in developing books and academic programs, especially in writing academic journals within the STEM field. Kimberley Blount, who holds a Diploma in English Language Teaching to Adults (Cambridge DELTA), made significant contributions to multiple aspects of the project. Leveraging her expertise, she played a role in not only writing Chapters 2 and 3 alongside Michael Brandon and Hugh Newton but also in proofreading, revising, and providing examples and scripts. The commitment, professional knowledge, and experience of the writers enabled the development team to successfully complete this project.

During the writing process, the review team–Yuah V. Chon, Kyungsook Kim, Hye-jin Hawkes, and Connie Park–devoted as much time as the writers to review the materials. The review process was conducted three times during the writing process to ensure the quality of the content. Connie Park and Hye-Jin Hawkes mainly reviewed and provided valuable feedback on the presentation part, while Yuah V. Chon, Kyungsook Kim, and Hye-Jin Hawkes focused on providing feedback on the writing part. The offering of their time and expertise in reviewing materials concurrently with writing enabled completing the project. Thus, their enormous contribution is highly appreciated.

The executive team was involved in not only making important decisions in the process of the entire book development process, but also served as the editorial team. After nearly 7 months of writing, reviewing and revising by the writers and reviewers, the executive team dedicated an additional four months to examine the entire material to check any missing elements, ensuring order of the content and unity in writing style. The executive team devoted many long hours to intensive meetings and discussions, meticulously refining the content of the book. The members of this team deserve recognition for their significant contributions. We offer our sincere thanks for their expertise: Yuah V. Chon, with her expertise in English Education, ESL, and textbook development theories; Kyungsook Kim who brought knowledge in TEFL and English Education; and Hye-Jin Hawkes, who contributed her skills in STEM, academic writing, and textbook development. The textbook team would especially like to thank Hye-Jin Hawkes for her hard work in developing the textbook. She coordinated the entire writing process through close communication with writers, reviewers, and executives as well as with Hanyang Press. Her past textbook development experience and dedication to the project made this possible.

We would also like to extend our special thanks to other contributors involved in the book development process. Ian Jones was involved in the brainstorming stage at the start of the process. His expertise in HASS was much appreciated when planning the content list of the book. Taeyong Park was extremely kind enough to offer his drawings for the textbook. It was a completely voluntary act and the drawings he created contributed greatly towards increasing the quality of the textbook. We would also like to thank Shelley Collins, Michael Brandon, Kyungsook Kim and Hye-Jin Hawkes for providing student essay samples. The sample essays will be a great help for students who learn academic writing skills through this book.

Last but not least, we extend our gratitude to the students who volunteered their essays and agreed to allow them to be refined and included in this book. Their essays were used either entirely or partially in the writing part as well as the appendix. These essay examples are the representation of how hard students worked to produce such outstanding essays. The list of essays that are used in this book is shown on the next page.

**Students**

| Essay type | Title of the essay | Student's name | Major |
|---|---|---|---|
| STEM | Pros and Cons of Drone Delivery | Taegun, Yang | Mechanical Engineering |
| STEM | The Advantages of Small Modular Reactors | Jiwon, Lim | Nuclear Engineering |
| HASS | Konglish Should be Accepted as a Dialect of English | Yoonseo, Kim | English Language & Literature |
| HASS | Revolutionizing Fashion Marketing: The Power of AI Technology | Chaerin, Kim | Clothing and Textiles |

Finally, we thank all the faculty members and professors in the College of English Education Committee for their moral support, encouragement and more importantly taking part in the textbook evaluation survey

'Academic Horizons: Skills Across Disciplines' textbook development team

## Contents

Chapter 3 | **PRESENTATION**



**Writing Appendix**



**Presentation Appendix**

Chapter 1

# RESEARCH AND INFORMATION GATHERING

*Writing an academic essay is very similar to cooking a meal. You cannot step into the kitchen and throw food together in the hope that it will turn into a delicious meal. There are steps that you need to follow: deciding what you would like to make, gathering the ingredients, carefully preparing them, and putting everything together to make your meal.*

This chapter will introduce steps for research and information gathering in writing an academic essay.

## 1. Brainstorming and Topic Generation

When writing an academic essay, you need to have a well-defined topic and a collection of ideas and perspectives. This preliminary phase, commonly known as **brainstorming**, involves the extraction of ideas from the depths of one's mind. The purpose is to narrow the focus and refine the topic for further exploration. There are three brainstorming techniques: **Free writing**, **Cluster**, and **Tree method**.

## 1.1. Free Writing Method

Find a quiet location where you can have a pen and paper or a mobile device at hand. Examine the chosen topic thoroughly, considering its various dimensions. Free writing serves the purpose of extracting all ideas without concern for spelling or grammar errors. Simply write down whatever thoughts come to mind. Set a time limit, perhaps ten minutes, to ensure sufficient brainstorming, and then proceed to arrange your thoughts by grouping related ideas under appropriate subheadings. In Figure 1.1, the writer brainstorms the different kinds of impact that 'Fast Fashion' may have on the environment, business, and consumers.

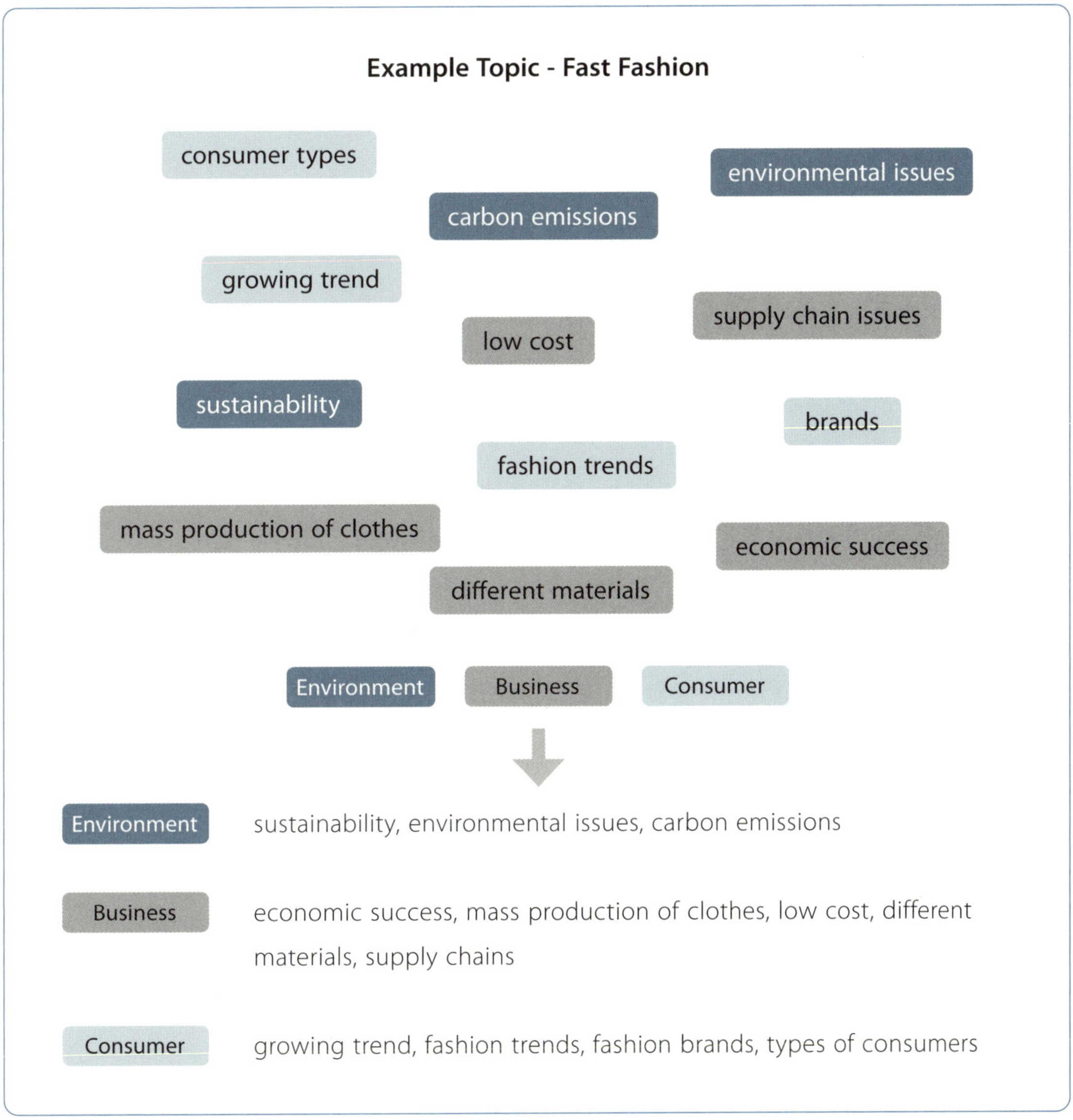


**Figure 1.1.** Free writing map

## 1.2. Cluster Method

Place your topic in the center of the page and generate as many diverse ideas as possible around it. Following that, start the process of connecting these ideas. Use visual representation to understand the relevance of each idea and create connections not only to the main topic but also among themselves. The aim of using visual representation for your ideas is to encourage interconnectedness both with the central

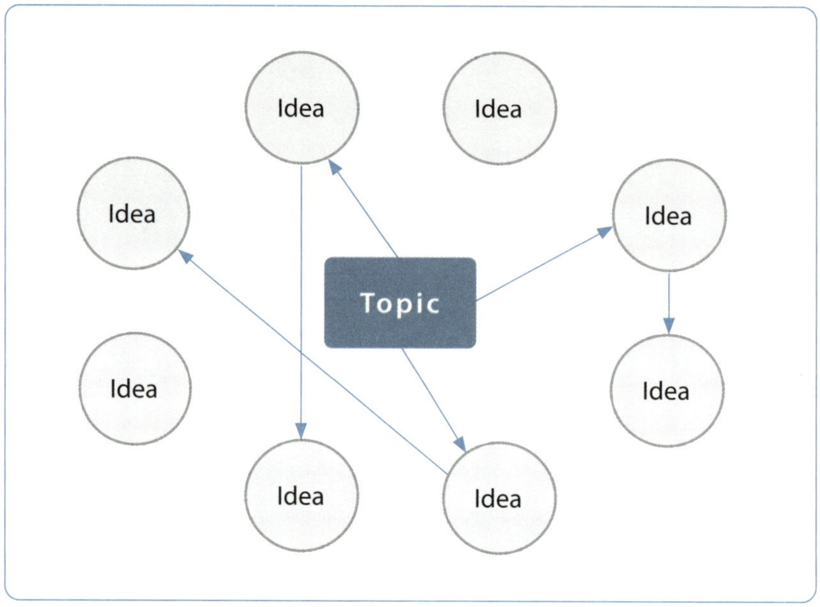


topic and among the ideas themselves. These connections will help create a smooth and logical flow in your writing.

## 1.3. Tree Method

The **Tree Method** is another approach for visually representing your ideas. Begin by placing your topic at the top of the page, and then branch out with sub-topics, establishing connections to the main topic. Link your ideas to the corresponding sub-

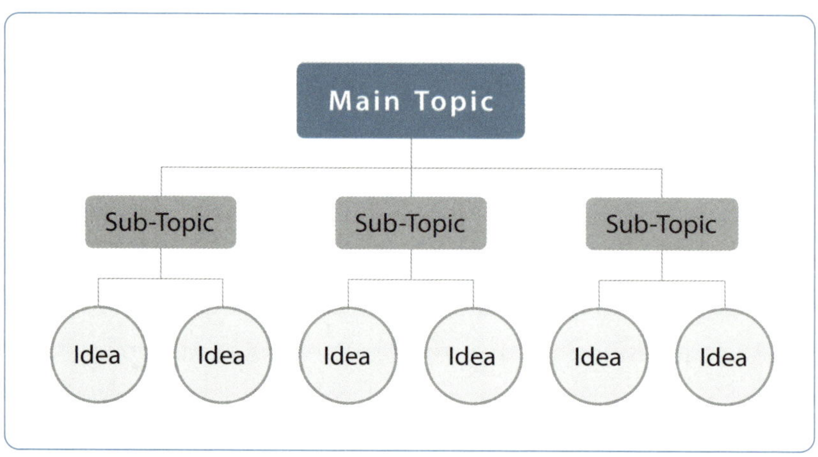

topics, aiming to generate a minimum of three connections for each. As you progress, your cluster of ideas will gradually take the form of a tree. This method enables you to interconnect your ideas in a more logical manner, thereby guiding the direction of your paper.

**TASK**

### Brainstorming Task

—

Choose a **Brainstorming Method** that you find the most interesting. Try to come up with a topic that you find exciting and brainstorm some ideas on that topic. Share your topic and ideas with your peers.

# 2. Research Reading Skills

In academic writing, it is crucial to support the chosen topic with evidence from reliable sources and authoritative figures in the respective field. This section will guide you on how to find and collect information to support the chosen topic appropriately.

## 2.1. What Are Reliable Sources?

For undergraduate students and those newly starting research, determining the reliability of sources can be challenging. Table 1.1. provides guidance in selecting the most appropriate sources for academic writing.

**Table 1.1.** Source types in academic writing

| Reliability | Source types |
|---|---|
| Strong | Books |
| | Journal Articles |
| | Creative Artwork |
| | Websites<br>• Education organizations (e.g., Universities)<br>• Government websites (including reports)<br>• Globally well-known non-profit organizations (e.g., WHO, NASA, UN etc.) |
| Somewhat strong<br>Somewhat weak | internationally well-known newspapers (BBC News, NY Times etc.) |
| | Magazines |
| | Commercial websites and reports |
| | Blogs |
| Very weak | Wiki |
| | Social media |

Having understood the significance of reliable sources, the next step is to explore methods and platforms for locating them.

University websites are a notable option, providing access to a wide range of credible sources. Additionally, the following list presents a collection of globally recognized search engines:

- Google Scholar – all disciplines:
  https://scholar.google.com/schhp?hl=en&as_sdt=0,5
- Pubmed – Medicine and Science:
  https://www.ncbi.nlm.nih.gov/pmc/
- World Wide Science – Science:
  https://worldwidescience.org/
- Science.gov. Your Gateway to U.S. Federal Science – Science:
  https://www.science.gov/
- Base – all majors:
  https://www.base-search.net/

• Infotopia – all majors:
https://www.infotopia.info/cuttleFish.html

## 2.2. Features of Reliable Sources

Many sources are available online, but it can be challenging to determine if they are reliable. While many are recognizable as to what type of sources they are, some are confusing. The following shows specific features of major sources.

### A. Books

[1] All books must contain a publisher.

Mewburn, I., Firth, K., & Lehmann, S. (2018). *How to Fix Your Academic Writing Trouble: A Practical Guide [Ebook].* McGraw-Hill Education (UK).

*Publisher* → McGraw-Hill Education

[2] Some e-books have a DOI number after a publisher.

Abu-Taieh, E. M. O., & El-Sheikh, A. A. (2010). *Handbook of research on discrete event simulation environments: Technologies and applications.* IGI Global. doi:10.4018/978-1-60566-774-4

*DOI number* → doi:10.4018/978-1-60566-774-4

[3] Some e-books have URL after a publisher.

Harris, P. (2002). *Designing and reporting experiments in psychology* (2nd ed.). McGraw Hill. http://www.mheducation.co.uk/openup/chapters/0335201466.pdf

*URL* → http://www.mheducation.co.uk/openup/chapters/0335201466.pdf

NOTE

## What is a **DOI**?

**DOI** stands for **Digital Object Identifier**, which contains numbers, letters, and symbols. It is just like an URL address of a website, but a **DOI** is mainly a URL for academic sources. Therefore, when you see it, you can find the permanent web address of a particular academic source. It is more often used for journal articles, which will be introduced in the next section.

### B. Journal articles

Most journal articles show distinguishable elements from books or other websites. Although there are some exceptions, most of them contain the following elements (Figure 1.2):

a. Title of article
b. Name of the journal
c. Volume or/and Issue numbers
d. Page numbers
e. DOI
f. Abstract

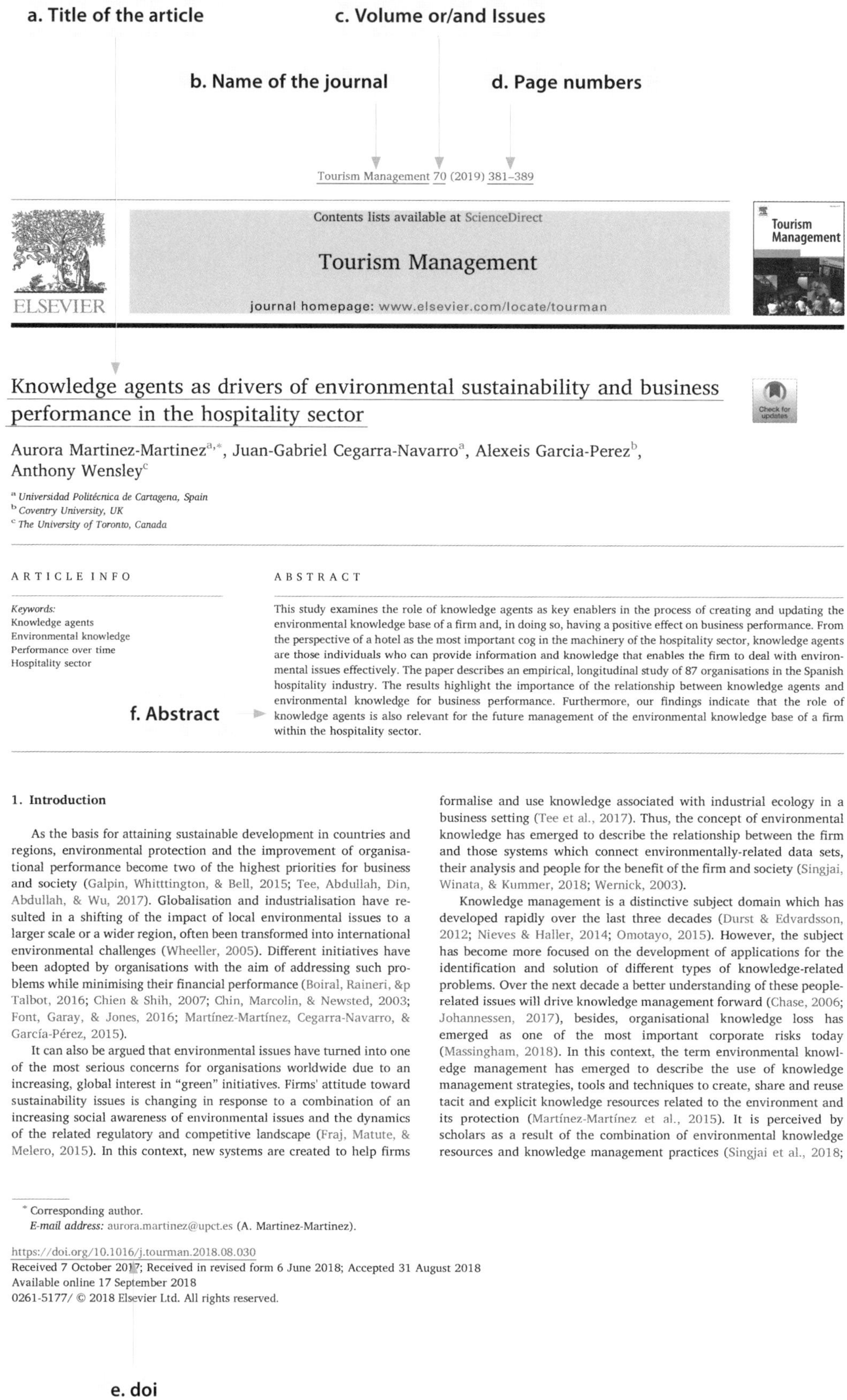


Tourism Management 70 (2019) 381–389

Contents lists available at ScienceDirect

Tourism Management

journal homepage: www.elsevier.com/locate/tourman

# Knowledge agents as drivers of environmental sustainability and business performance in the hospitality sector

Aurora Martinez-Martinez[a,*], Juan-Gabriel Cegarra-Navarro[a], Alexeis Garcia-Perez[b], Anthony Wensley[c]

[a] Universidad Politécnica de Cartagena, Spain
[b] Coventry University, UK
[c] The University of Toronto, Canada

ARTICLE INFO

*Keywords:*
Knowledge agents
Environmental knowledge
Performance over time
Hospitality sector

ABSTRACT

This study examines the role of knowledge agents as key enablers in the process of creating and updating the environmental knowledge base of a firm and, in doing so, having a positive effect on business performance. From the perspective of a hotel as the most important cog in the machinery of the hospitality sector, knowledge agents are those individuals who can provide information and knowledge that enables the firm to deal with environmental issues effectively. The paper describes an empirical, longitudinal study of 87 organisations in the Spanish hospitality industry. The results highlight the importance of the relationship between knowledge agents and environmental knowledge for business performance. Furthermore, our findings indicate that the role of knowledge agents is also relevant for the future management of the environmental knowledge base of a firm within the hospitality sector.

## 1. Introduction

As the basis for attaining sustainable development in countries and regions, environmental protection and the improvement of organisational performance become two of the highest priorities for business and society (Galpin, Whitttington, & Bell, 2015; Tee, Abdullah, Din, Abdullah, & Wu, 2017). Globalisation and industrialisation have resulted in a shifting of the impact of local environmental issues to a larger scale or a wider region, often been transformed into international environmental challenges (Wheeller, 2005). Different initiatives have been adopted by organisations with the aim of addressing such problems while minimising their financial performance (Boiral, Raineri, &p Talbot, 2016; Chien & Shih, 2007; Chin, Marcolin, & Newsted, 2003; Font, Garay, & Jones, 2016; Martínez-Martínez, Cegarra-Navarro, & García-Pérez, 2015).

It can also be argued that environmental issues have turned into one of the most serious concerns for organisations worldwide due to an increasing, global interest in "green" initiatives. Firms' attitude toward sustainability issues is changing in response to a combination of an increasing social awareness of environmental issues and the dynamics of the related regulatory and competitive landscape (Fraj, Matute, & Melero, 2015). In this context, new systems are created to help firms formalise and use knowledge associated with industrial ecology in a business setting (Tee et al., 2017). Thus, the concept of environmental knowledge has emerged to describe the relationship between the firm and those systems which connect environmentally-related data sets, their analysis and people for the benefit of the firm and society (Singjai, Winata, & Kummer, 2018; Wernick, 2003).

Knowledge management is a distinctive subject domain which has developed rapidly over the last three decades (Durst & Edvardsson, 2012; Nieves & Haller, 2014; Omotayo, 2015). However, the subject has become more focused on the development of applications for the identification and solution of different types of knowledge-related problems. Over the next decade a better understanding of these people-related issues will drive knowledge management forward (Chase, 2006; Johannessen, 2017), besides, organisational knowledge loss has emerged as one of the most important corporate risks today (Massingham, 2018). In this context, the term environmental knowledge management has emerged to describe the use of knowledge management strategies, tools and techniques to create, share and reuse tacit and explicit knowledge resources related to the environment and its protection (Martínez-Martínez et al., 2015). It is perceived by scholars as a result of the combination of environmental knowledge resources and knowledge management practices (Singjai et al., 2018;

* Corresponding author.
*E-mail address:* aurora.martinez@upct.es (A. Martinez-Martinez).

https://doi.org/10.1016/j.tourman.2018.08.030
Received 7 October 2017; Received in revised form 6 June 2018; Accepted 31 August 2018
Available online 17 September 2018


**Figure 1.2.** Key elements of a journal article

### C. Education and Government Organizations

Materials that are published in education and government organisations are considered reliable.

a. Educational organizations: a web address which ends with .edu or .ac
https://news.harvard.edu/gazette/story/2022/06/200m-gift-to-fund-harvard-climate-crisis-institute/

b. Governments: a web address which ends with .gov
https://www.hhs.gov/programs/prevention-and-wellness/nutrition-and-fitness/index.html

### D. Globally Well-known Non-profit Organizations

Non-profit organizations use their web address with org. at the end of its URL. However, **NOT ALL** non-profit organizations are considered '**reliable**' for academic writing. How do you find 'reliable' sources, then? One way is to recognize the '**reputation**' of an organization. For example, the **World Health Organization (WHO)** or the **United Nations (UN)** are well-known organizations worldwide, and their reputations are very high. During the COVID-19 pandemic, the **WHO** released the COVID-19 related guidelines, and most countries followed them. This shows the trustworthiness of their publications.

***TASK***

Using a topic that you have chosen from brainstorming, search for three reliable sources (one of each type) using the search engines introduced above.

| Sources | What did you find?<br>(Write the web address you found) |
|---|---|
| Book | |
| Journal article | |
| Reliable websites | |

## 2.3. Reading Strategy

Once you have acquired skills to find reliable sources, the next step is to read the sources effectively to use them in your writing.

### A. CRAAP

The **CRAAP** test is a set of criteria used to evaluate the credibility and relevance of sources. The acronym "**CRAAP**" stands for:

#### Currency: date of publication

- When was the information published or posted?
- Does your topic require current information, or will older sources be ok?

#### Relevance: how related the information is for your essay

- How well does the information support your essay?
- Would this information strengthen your essay?

#### Authority: information on creator's or publisher's credentials

- Who or what organization created or published the information?
- What credentials (education, affiliations, experience) do they have on this topic?

#### Accuracy: evidence supported information

- Is the information factual?
- What evidence is used to support the information?
- Does the language or tone seem objective and free of emotion?

#### Purpose: the reason the information exists

- Why was the information written and published (e.g., to inform, teach, entertain, persuade)?
- Is there potential bias? (If someone who is working for a biotech company publishes an article for his company, there is a high probability that it is biased.)

TASK

CRAAP Test

—

Does your source pass the test? If the answer is 'yes' to all of the following, then it is good to use for your essay.

| | | |
|---|---|---|
| **Currency** | Publication date is acceptable | Yes / No |
| **Relevance** | The information is relevant to my topic | Yes / No |
| **Authority** | Author has expert credentials and/or the source is known, published, and reputable | Yes / No |
| **Accuracy** | Evidence supported information | Yes / No |
| **Purpose** | Author bias not exhibited | Yes / No |

## B. Abstracts

- Location: On the first page of a journal article
- Length: 200-250 words

It is highly recommended to read the abstract first before reading the entire journal article. The abstract is a summary of a journal article offering insights into the article's main focus and highlighting key information. When selecting sources for an assignment, reading the abstract in each article can save a significant amount of time. Within just a few minutes, it is often possible to assess whether further reading of the article is worthwhile.

### C. Annotation

Annotation is another useful and valuable skill in research reading, and here are **four** strategies.

- **Highlight**: When you read, consider highlighting, underlining, or circling important key terms or points. You can use different color codes to distinguish which one is the most and least important.
- **Numbers**: Use numbers to indicate the order in which phrases, sentences, or paragraphs will be used in your writing.
- **Summary**: If you plan to incorporate paragraph(s) or even an entire section from a source, create a summary in your own words in a separate file, distinct from your actual writing.
- **Paraphrase**: If you intend to use only a few sentences, be sure to paraphrase them to prevent plagiarism.

* An annotation template is provided in Appendix 1.

## 3. Integrating Sources

When composing an academic essay, it is vital to support your argument using evidence. There are three methods of integrating evidence into your writing: **Quoting**, **Paraphrasing**, and **Summarizing**.

| | |
|---|---|
| **Quoting** | • Borrowing exact words from outside sources with quotation marks "..."<br>• Make sure to indicate the source |
| **Paraphrasing** | • Restating ideas from a source using your own words<br>• Make sure to indicate the source |
| **Summarizing** | • Condensing a large amount of information into a brief explanation in your own words<br>• Make sure to indicate the source |

Chapter 2

# WRITING

*"If you want to be a writer, you must do two things above all others: read a lot and write a lot."*

*- Stephen King*

## 1. Introduction to Academic Writing

Academic writing is a formal type of writing that is used by scholars, researchers, and students in universities and other academic institutions to communicate their ideas and research findings. Distinctive characteristics include a formal tone, precise word choices, use of predominantly third-person perspective, and a clear focus on an issue or research problem.

This chapter will specifically focus on academic writing in two major university disciplines: Science, Technology, Engineering and Mathematics (STEM) and Humanities, Arts and Social Sciences (HASS) since there are distinctive differences in academic writing between STEM and HASS (Table 2.1).

**Table 2.1.** Distinctive features of STEM and HASS writing

| Aspect | STEM | HASS |
|---|---|---|
| **Purpose** | Inform and present research findings | Analyze, interpret, and critique |
| **Writing Style** | Formal, precise, and objective | Varied, and may include personal voice and opinions |
| **Writing Process** | Emphasizes empirical evidence and analysis | Focuses on critical thinking and interpretation |
| **Language** | Emphasizes technical terminology | Balances use of technical and descriptive terms |
| **Citation Style** | Often uses the Institute of Electrical and Electronics Engineers (IEEE) or American Psychological Association (APA) | Primarily uses the American Psychological Association (APA) or Modern Language Association (MLA) |

To create an academic essay, careful planning and specific skills are required. For high-quality academic writing, there are several steps to follow (Figure 2.1). The first two stages, 1. Choosing a topic and 2. Brainstorming, were discussed in Chapter 1. This chapter will present the remaining stages.

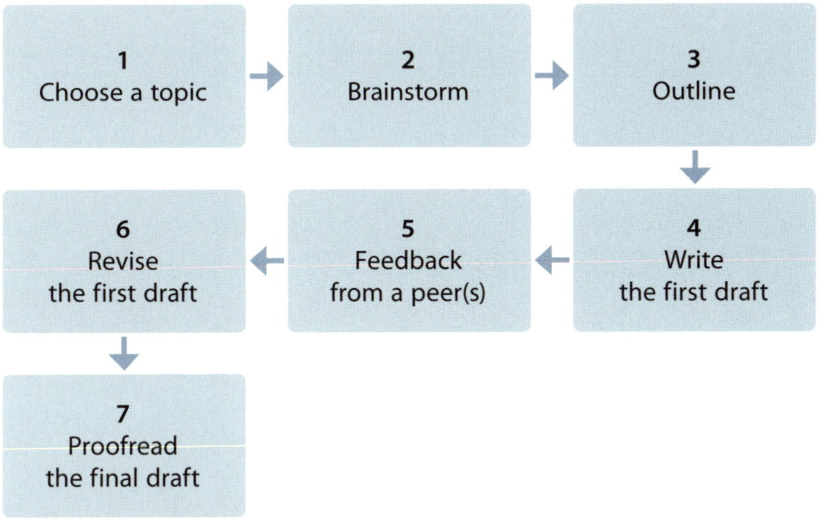


**Figure 2.1.** Writing stages of an academic essay

# 2. The Writing Process

- **Learn** the most common essay structure from the five-paragraph essay model.
- **Learn** how to write an introduction, body, and conclusion as required in academic writing. This includes an introductory paragraph, body paragraphs to develop and support main ideas, and a concluding paragraph.

## 2.1. Essay Structure

Before writing an essay, it is necessary to understand the essay structure to help you see a big picture of an academic essay.

## Success of Australia's Tourism

**INTRODUCTION**

Background

Thesis statement

Many successful industries contribute to the GDP of Australia. One such industry, the tourism industry, contributes 3.2 per cent to Australia's income and is responsible for employing 4.9 per cent of the population (Department of Resources, Energy and Tourism, 2020). Australia, a land of contrasts and wonders, has consistently been a magnet for travelers worldwide. From the iconic Sydney Opera House and the Great Barrier Reef to the mysteries of the Outback, the country offers a range of attractions that few places can match. While its popularity among tourists is undeniable, pinpointing the exact reasons for this appeal requires a closer look. The success of Australia's tourism can be attributed to breathtaking landscapes and unique wildlife.

**Body**
**(Body Paragraph 1)**

Topic sentence

Supporting sentences

Concluding sentence

Australia's unique geological and ecological features make it a particularly attractive tourist location. First, Australia's Tourism Commissioner states that 67% of tourists from 2010 to 2014 cited extraordinary natural phenomena as a significant motivating reason for their visit (Figure 1) (DRET, 2020). For example, the Uluru-Kata Tjuta National Park is listed as one of the few World Heritage properties recognized for both its natural and cultural values (Georgiou, 2017, p. 21). Uluru is acknowledged as the world's largest monolith (DRET, 2020), and the formation is so rare that it captivates the world with its sheer size, vibrant colors, and cultural significance. Another reason that Australia is attractive to overseas tourists is that it has over 10,000 miles of white sandy beaches, some of the world's best surfing conditions and a climate that allows comfortable swimming throughout the year (DRET, 2020). Unique geological features and ecology create landforms which are key components of Australia's appeal to tourists.

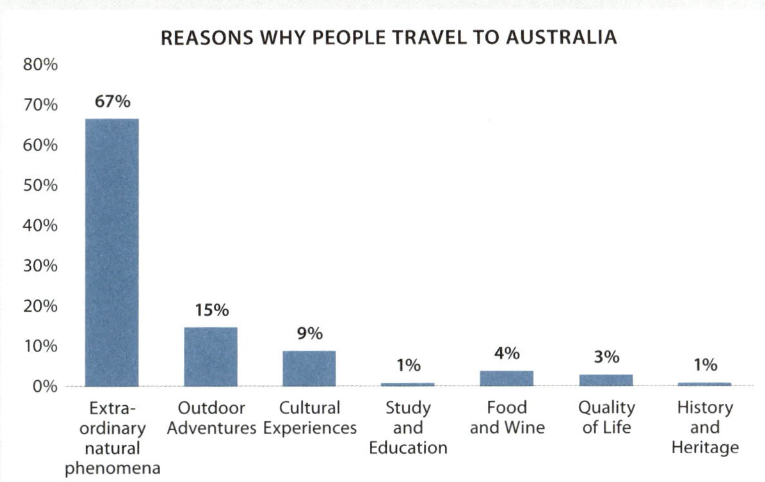


**Figure 1.** Reasons why people travel to Australia

.......................... **(Body Paragraph 2)**

.......................... **(Body Paragraph 3)**

In conclusion, Australia's immense appeal to tourists arises from its unparalleled geological features and diverse wildlife. While the nation benefits substantially from the tourism sector, the challenges of the geographic distance from major global hubs were not discussed in this essay. Also, the research was limited to the years 2010 to 2014, and a broader timeframe may offer varied insights. Future research could examine evolving tourist preferences, especially in the post-pandemic era, and assess the potential impact of virtual tourism. Ultimately, despite its remoteness, Australia's ability to provide a unique, consolidated experience ensures tourists find the journey worth their time and resources.

**CONCLUSION**
Summary

Limit of research

Future research plan

Final comment

**References**


Brown, J. M., & Parker, R. E. (2017). Australia's distinctive land creatures: A comprehensive guide. *Journal of Wildlife Research, 42*(3), 211-226. https://doi.org/10.105/j.wr.2017.32.03

Department of Resources, Energy and Tourism (DRET) (2020), *Australia tourism and overseas statistics and status.* Retrieved https://arena.gov.au/funding/department-of-resources-energy-and-tourism/

Georgiou, A. A. (2007). The most attractive tourist areas in Australia. *Journal of Australian Tourism, 4*(5), 43-49. https://doi.org/10.3459 64kl30298as


**REFERENCE LIST**

This example essay is written in the common five-paragraph format used for academic essays.

### A. Introductory Paragraph

The introduction is the first 'meeting point' with the readers. The introductory paragraph should accomplish two goals: (1) capturing the reader's interest and (2) introducing the essay's topic. The introduction in an academic essay usually includes background information and a thesis statement.

**Table 2.2.** Structure of an Introductory Paragraph

| Title: Success of Australia's Tourism | |
|---|---|
| **General Background Information** | Many successful industries contribute to the GDP of Australia. One such industry, the tourism industry, contributes 3.2 per cent to Australia's income and is responsible for employing 4.9 per cent of the population (Department of Resources, Energy and Tourism, 2020). |
| **Specific Background Information** | Australia, a land of contrasts and wonders, has consistently been a magnet for travelers worldwide. From the iconic Sydney Opera House and the Great Barrier Reef to the mysteries of the Outback, the country offers a range of attractions that few places can match. While its popularity among tourists is undeniable, pinpointing the exact reasons for this appeal requires a closer look. |
| **Thesis Statement** | The success of Australia's tourism can be attributed to breathtaking landscapes and unique wildlife. |

### a. Background Information

The purpose of **background information** is to set the scene for the essay topic. It should be written with a focus on connecting the background information to the thesis statement. Therefore, your ideas about the topic will progress from **general** to **specific information**.

- General Background: When you start your essay, make sure to give general information about the topic.

**Specific Background Information (This means narrowing the content to the thesis statement)**: Provide information that establishes more specific foundation and background content for the essay. Reveal your **stance on the topic** by addressing issues, concerns, causes, effects, problems, analysis, or descriptions of a particular phenomenon or event. To write this effectively, the following options are commonly used:

- **Definition**: Define a particular term that is highly related to your topic.
- **History**: Provide a short history or past that is related to your topic.
- **Statistics**: Provide specific data or statistics that are related to your topic.
- **Status**: Discuss the status of a certain aspect that is related to your topic.
- **Facts**: Search secondary sources to provide an interesting fact or story that connects to your topic.

**TASK**

- Read a sentence in the General Background section in Table 2.2 on the previous page. Compare it with the title and thesis statement. Is it general enough? Why or why not? If you think it can be better, improve it.
- Read the Specific Background Information section in Table 2.2 Compare it with the title. Is it highly related to the topic? Can you see the writer's stance through this section? If you think this part can be better, improve it.

**NOTE**

## STEM

In scientific writing, it is extremely important to include **sources** in the introduction. Since a scientific essay is based on collection of facts, the writer's stance must be supported by external sources. The introduction is the best place to add them. **Add them as appropriate.**

### b. Thesis Statement

A **thesis statement** clearly expresses the central argument or claim of an essay or research paper. It serves as a roadmap to guide the reader through the main points and supporting evidence. To illustrate the difference between effective and less effective thesis statements, compare the following examples:

**Weak Thesis Statement**: Air pollution is bad.

**Strong Thesis Statement**: Rapid urban industrialization has increased air pollution, posing three health risks that demand local government intervention.

### A thesis statement includes:

**[Topic] + [Claim] + [Supporting Points]**

**Topic**: What the essay is about.
**Claim**: What you believe or are arguing about the topic.
**Supporting Points**: Brief reasons or evidence that will be explored in the body of your essay to support your claim.

*Example*
**Topic**: The effects of online learning
**Claim**: Online learning has significant advantages
**Supporting Points**: Flexibility in scheduling, diverse course offerings, and personalized pacing

**Thesis Statement**: Online learning offers significant advantages, including flexibility in scheduling, a diverse range of courses, and the ability for students to pace themselves.

**TASK**

Identify topic, claim, and supporting points in the following thesis statement:

*The impact of social media on mental health, particularly among adolescents, is profound, as it influences self-esteem, social interactions, and overall well-being.*

## B. Body Paragraphs

An academic essay consists of two or more body paragraphs that expand on the thesis statement introduced in the introduction. The number of main ideas you have for the essay will determine the number of paragraphs you write in the body section. Each paragraph should focus on one main idea, which should be followed by supporting sentences.

### a. Topic Sentences

**A topic sentence** introduces the main idea of a paragraph. It is recommended to be one sentence and located at the beginning of a paragraph. A **topic sentence** is composed of a **topic** and a **controlling idea**.

**Topic + Controlling idea** = **Topic Sentence**

**Topic**: It is usually made up of a few key words, and it introduces the main idea of the paragraph.
**Controlling idea**: This part of the topic sentence is the specific point, opinion, or argument that the writer wants to make about the topic.

The purpose of the controlling idea is...

- To specify which particular aspect of the topic will be discussed in the paragraph.
- To limit or control the type of information that will be discussed in that paragraph.

*Examples*

The first area of concern regarding GMO use is ← *Topic*
the prospective detrimental impact on the environment. ← *Controlling idea*

One of the distinctive characteristics of Australia for tourists is ← *Topic*
its unique geological and ecological features. ← *Controlling idea*

**TASK**

Read the following topic sentences. Circle the topic and underline the controlling idea.

- Three of the largest and worst slums in the world include Cairo, Port au Prince, and Tondo.
- People living in shanty towns experience the detrimental health effects of sub-standard living conditions.
- VR has been used in the healthcare system and there are two reasons why.

**NOTE**

In a 'well-written' essay, topic sentences are…

- well connected to the **thesis statement** in the introduction.
- included in each paragraph and fully developed in the **supporting sentences**.
- restated effectively in the **conclusion**.

### b. Supporting Sentences

**Supporting sentences** will provide additional details, explanations, and evidence to support the main idea introduced in the topic sentence. Supporting sentences expand on the controlling idea and help to develop the paragraph by providing specific examples, details, or arguments that support or prove the writer's point.

| | |
|---|---|
| Australia's unique geological and ecological features make it a particularly attractive tourist location. | **Body** **(Body Paragraph 1)** Topic sentence |
| First, Australia's Tourism Commissioner states that 67% of tourists from 2010 to 2014 cited extraordinary natural phenomena as a significant motivating reason for their visit (Figure 1) (DRET, 2020). For example, the Uluru-Kata Tjuta National Park is listed as one of the few World Heritage properties recognized for both its natural and cultural values (Georgiou, 2017, p. 21). Uluru is acknowledged as the world's largest monolith (DRET, 2020), and the formation is so rare that it captivates the world with its sheer size, vibrant colors, and cultural significance. Another reason that Australia is attractive to overseas tourists is that it has over 10,000 miles of white sandy beaches, some of the world's best surfing conditions and a climate that allows comfortable swimming throughout the year (DRET, 2020). | Supporting sentences |
| Unique geological features and ecology create landforms which are key components of Australia's appeal to tourists. | Concluding sentence |

**Figure 1.** Reasons why people travel to Australia

**Table 2.3.** Distinctive features of the body paragraphs between STEM and HASS essays

| Aspect | STEM | HASS |
|---|---|---|
| **Objective vs. Subjective** | Emphasizes objectivity and neutrality | Allows for subjectivity and personal interpretation |
| **Use of Personal Pronouns** | Generally avoids personal pronouns (e.g., I) | May use personal pronouns (e.g., I, we) |
| **Tone** | Formal, technical, and precise | Varies depending on sub-discipline or argument |
| **Citation Style and References** | Emphasizes authoritative sources | May include a wider range of sources and genres compared with STEM |

As can be seen in Table 2.3, there are also key differences when writing supporting sentences between STEM and HASS academic writing.

#### c. Concluding Sentences

A **concluding sentence** provides a sense of closure in a paragraph. To write an effective concluding sentence, either restate the topic sentence through paraphrasing or create a smooth transition to the next paragraph.

***Example***

Topic sentence: Australia's unique geological and ecological features make it a particularly attractive tourist location.

↓

Concluding sentence:

- **Restatement**: Unique geological features and ecology create landforms which are key components of Australia's appeal to tourists.
- **Transition**: With its captivating geological wonders, Australia also provides an extraordinary habitat for an unparalleled diversity of wildlife.

### C. Concluding Paragraph

To effectively end the essay, it is important to summarize the key points of the essay as it is the last chance to impress the reader. Therefore, by simply reading the conclusion, the reader should be able to understand the main topic of the essay and the key points that were explored to address it. An effective conclusion consists of:

- **Summary/Restatement**: do not repeat the thesis statement or topic sentences but paraphrase your thesis and reiterate the main ideas clearly.

- **Limit of research**
  1. Analyze your own essay.
  2. Recognize shortcomings of your own essay.
- **Future research plan**
  1. Future research plan(s) can be related to shortcomings of your essay.
  2. Introduce a future research plan as if you would perform further research if a chance were given.
- **Final comment**: It is an opportunity to express your opinion or stance by discussing why the thesis of the essay is important. A final comment should **not** be a general comment, but it should tie back to your thesis and provide a thoughtful, reflective, or critical viewpoint that leaves a lasting impression on the reader.

| | |
|---|---|
| In conclusion, Australia's immense appeal to tourists arises from its unparalleled geological features and diverse wildlife. | Summary |
| While the nation benefits substantially from the tourism sector, the challenges of the geographic distance from major global hubs were not discussed in this essay. Also, the research was limited to the years 2010 to 2014, and a broader timeframe may offer varied insights. | Limit of research |
| Future research could examine evolving tourist preferences, especially in the post-pandemic era, and assess the potential impact of virtual tourism. | Future research plan |
| Ultimately, despite its remoteness, Australia's ability to provide a unique, consolidated experience ensures tourists find the journey worth their time and resources. | Final comment |

### Limit of research and future research plan

***Example***

*Limit of research* → However, this essay only focused on the positive aspects of GM crops, while they can induce immune reactions and cause serious allergies.

*Future research plan* → Therefore, it is necessary to further study the negative aspects of GM crops.

### Final Comment

***Example***

If the government took these steps, the result would be a safer, healthier environment for people living in these areas.

### D. Reference List

At the end of an essay, the sources used must be listed on a new page. The Reference List should include the author(s), title(s), publication company, URL or DOI, publication date, and other relevant information (more information in 3.4).

***Example of a Reference List***

**References**

Brown, J. M., & Parker, R. E. (2017). Australia's distinctive land creatures: A comprehensive guide. *Journal of Wildlife Research, 42*(3), 211-226. https://doi.org/10.105/j.wr.2017.32.03

Department of Resources, Energy and Tourism. (DRET) (2020). *Australia tourism and overseas statistics and status*. https://arena.gov.au/funding/department-of-resources-energy-and-tourism/

Georgiou, A. A. (2007). The most attractive tourist areas in Australia. *Journal of Australian Tourism, 4*(5), 43-49. https://doi.org/10.345964kl30298as

## 2.2. Making an Outline

### A. Organizing ideas into an outline

**An outline** is a logical and chronological map for a writer to write an essay. Without it, it is easy for the writer to go off track and lose the focus of the topic.

Writing an outline offers several great benefits:

- An outline helps the writer be clear about how many main ideas will be developed into topic sentences.
- An outline helps ensure that the main ideas are **well-connected** to both the thesis and to each other.

- An outline helps the writer stay **focused** on the topic and main ideas.

### What is the best way to write an **outline**?

a. **Be concise**: Use phrases or short sentence(s).

b. **Be explicit**: Use keywords to be specific.

c. **Reference**: Consider academic sources that support your points.

### What should be included in the outline?

**Title**: XXXXXXXXXXXX

**Introduction**:

- Background information of the topic
- Thesis statement: main idea statement for the whole essay

**Body**:

» Topic sentence

- 2 or 3 Supporting details

» Topic sentence

- 2 or 3 Supporting details

» Topic sentence

- 2 or 3 Supporting details

**Conclusion**:

1. Summary of the main ideas/Restatement of the thesis statement
2. Limit of research
3. Future research plan
4. Final comment

## B. Writing An Outline

Write an outline of your essay using the model outline.

**TASK**

**Title**: Success of Australia's Tourism

**Introduction**:

- Tourism → 3.2% of Australia's income; tourist locations

**Thesis statement**: The success of Australia's tourism can be attributed to breathtaking landscapes and unique wildlife.

**Body**:

1. Breathtaking landscapes
   a. Uluru: the world's largest stone
   b. 10,000 miles of white sandy beaches

2. Unique wildlife
   a. the Great Barrier Reef: the second most popular tourist destination in Australia
   b. Australian animals: kangaroos and koalas

3. Dealing with counterarguments
   a. Stay 3 times longer than other countries
   b. As a result, spend more money in Australia

**Conclusion**:

1. Summary/Restatement
2. Limit of research: challenges due to the geographic distance and a narrow timeframe of the research data
3. Future research: examine tourist preferences (post-pandemic era), and assess the potential impact of virtual tourism
4. Final comment: provide a unique, consolidated experience to tourists

**Title**: ______________________________

**Introduction**: ______________________________

**Thesis statement**: ______________________________

**Body**:

1. Topic Sentence:

2. Topic Sentence:

3. Topic Sentence:

**Conclusion**:

1. Summary/Restatement

   : ______________________________

2. Limit of research

   : ______________________________

3. Future research plan

   : ______________________________

4. Final comment

   : ______________________________

# 3. Integrating and Crediting Sources

Academic writing requires incorporation of external sources with proper citation. This not only provides weight and authority to your arguments but also demonstrates your engagement with existing research. This section will explore the process of integrating external information with your own ideas, and how to cite sources appropriately to maintain scholarly credibility.

## 3.1. Using and Analyzing Sources

To support the writer's own views effectively, it is important to include research evidence and this section will discuss ways to do that.

### A. Integrating Sources

There are three different ways to introduce outside sources into an academic essay: **Quoting**, **paraphrasing**, and **summarizing**.

Each one has a different purpose and uses a different writing technique, so it is important that the writer understands which method is appropriate for supporting their points.

**NOTE**

When introducing information from sources, **signal phrases** are used and common examples include:

**according to, acknowledge, argue, believe,**
**claim, conclude, confirm, insist, illustrate, report**

- **According to** by the World Health Organization, regular exercise is essential for maintaining good health.
- Researchers **acknowledge** the limitations of their study, noting the small sample size.
- Smith and Lee **argue** that climate change impacts are accelerating faster than previously estimated.
- Many scientists **believe** that renewable energy sources are key to sustainable development.
- The author **claims** that implementing new policies can reduce carbon emissions significantly.
- The study **concludes** that diet has a major impact on heart health.
- Recent experiments **confirm** the theory's predictions about chemical reactions.
- Despite the criticism, the politician **insists** that the new policy will benefit the economy.
- The author uses numerous examples to **illustrate** the importance of cultural diversity.
- The study **reports** a significant increase in the use of renewable energy in the past decade.

### a. Quoting

Quoting, also known as direct quoting, refers to using the exact words of the original material. Direct quoting is used when the precise wording of the source material is important, such as when you want to preserve the author's unique style, language or terminology. Make sure to place double quotation marks (" ") around the quoted material with the page number.

*Example*

According to Gershwin (2019), there is "an inherent danger in not understanding the ramifications of A.I technology" (p. 26).

**NOTE**

A quote usually does not exceed one or two sentences from the original source to avoid the risk of losing the writer's own voice in the writing.

### b. Paraphrasing

Paraphrasing is the process of rephrasing or restating someone's writing or speech in your own words. It can also be used to simplify complex content or clarify ambiguous statements by expressing them in a clearer way. When paraphrasing other's ideas, concepts, or information, it is important not to alter the original meaning or misrepresent the author's intent. Proper referencing is also crucial to avoid plagiarism.

Five steps for effective paraphrasing

a) Read the original text carefully to understand the author's message and the key ideas correctly.
b) Identify technical terms that should be kept and other general English words that can be replaced with synonyms.
c) Substitute those common English terms with **synonyms**, rearrange **word order**, alter **voice**, and modify **sentence structure**.
d) Ensure that the original meaning of the source text is kept and that your own opinion is not added.
e) Include the citation.

*Example*

**Original**: The use of technology in education is far advanced with the emergence of artificial intelligence (AI), a system where machines are designed to mimic humans (Tahiru, 2021).

↓

**Subsitute with Synonyms**: The utilization of technology in academia has greatly progressed with the rise of artificial intelligence (AI), a framework in which machines are crafted to imitate humans (Tahiru, 2021).

↓

**Rearrange the word order**: With the rise of artificial intelligence (AI), a framework in which machines are crafted to imitate humans, the utilization of technology in academia has greatly progressed (Tahiru, 2021).

↓

**Alter voice**: With the rise of artificial intelligence (AI), a framework in which machines are crafted to imitate humans, significant progress has been made in the utilization of technology in academia (Tahiru, 2021).

↓

**Modify Sentence Structure**: Artificial intelligence (AI) has greatly progressed the utilization of technology in academia by creating a framework in which machines imitate humans (Tahiru, 2021).

**NOTE**

Compare the correct paraphrase with the incorrect paraphrase (i.e., distortion).

- **Original**: The rapid advancement of technology has revolutionized communication.
- **Correct paraphrase**: Communication has undergone a revolution due to the swift progress of technology.
- **Incorrect Paraphrase**: The fast-paced progression of technology has completely transformed how people communicate.

### c. Summarizing

Summarizing involves extracting key points from a source and presenting them in your own words, similar to paraphrasing. However, summarizing goes further by condensing larger portions, such as entire articles or book chapters, into a concise form while preserving the original meaning of the source text. Proper referencing is essential to give credit to the original author.

Five steps for effective summarizing:

a) Read the original text carefully to understand the author's message and the key ideas correctly.
b) Make memos of the key points using your own words.
c) Write a summary from the memos without referring to the original.
d) Check if your summary has covered the content and meaning of the original text correctly.
e) Include the citation.

***Example***

**Original**: The increasing number of internal-combustion vehicles which consume unrenewable conventional fuels has caused both energy and environmental issues [1]. Therefore, many countries have implemented new energy vehicles (NEVs) as alternatives to conventional vehicles to reduce the dependence on oil and air pollution caused by conventional vehicles [2,3,4]. As the world's largest automotive market, China has been committed to promoting NEVs to reduce the consumption and import of oil [3,5,6]. In Europe, Germany proposes to have one million EVs in operation by 2020 to reduce CO2 emissions [7,8,9]; France and UK have also aimed to restrict the in-country sale of conventional vehicles by 2040 [2]. To stimulate the adoption of NEVs, many countries offered subsidies and special tax policies, such as plug-in vehicle subsidies in the
UK, the clean vehicle rebate project in the US, and the green

vehicle purchasing promotion measures in Japan and China [10]. NEVs that use unconventional energy to power vehicles mainly include electric vehicles (EVs), hydrogen vehicles, natural gas vehicles, methanol and ethanol vehicles. Among these NEVs, EVs are considered as the most effective to achieve environmental and socioeconomic benefits [11] [Source: Sun, X., Li, Z., Wang, X., & Li, C. (2019). Technology development of electric vehicles: A review. *Energies, 13*(1), 90. **https://doi.org/10.3390/en13010090**]

**Summary**: The rise in internal-combustion vehicles fueled by non-renewable resources has led to energy and environmental challenges, prompting many nations to adopt new energy vehicles (NEVs) with various incentives. Among others, EVs are widely recognized as the most effective choice for achieving environmental and socioeconomic benefits [1-11].

### B. Avoiding Plagiarism

When using sources to support the writer's opinion, it is important to cite them properly. Plagiarism is the act of presenting others' ideas and opinions as your own without giving them the necessary credit, and it is considered dishonest. Take note of different forms of plagiarism explained below and try to avoid them for academic integrity.

#### a. Assignment Plagiarism

This includes using assignments written by others as your own. An example of this could be downloading an already completed essay from the Internet or paying another person to write the essay for you.

#### b. Direct Plagiarism

This is the most straightforward form of plagiarism. This occurs when you copy sentences, paragraphs, or entire sections from a source without acknowledging where the information came from.

### c. Indirect Plagiarism

This happens when you paraphrase someone else's writing by changing some key words and phrases without providing citations, while keeping the main intention of the original source. Again, since no citation is provided, this still counts as plagiarism.

### d. Patchwork Plagiarism

This form of plagiarism happens when a writer takes sentences from different parts of another writers' work and weaves them together to make it appear as if the ideas are wholly the writer's own.

### e. Accidental Plagiarism

Plagiarism can still occur even if you did not have the intention to commit it. This happens when the writer simply forgets to cite their sources correctly. Make sure to include a citation every time you use outside sources in your writing.

## 3.2. Engaging with Counterarguments and Limitations

### A. Dealing with Counterarguments

In academic writing, addressing counterarguments is important to construct persuasive arguments. It demonstrates the writer's awareness of diverse viewpoints and strengthens the argument by challenging opposing perspectives.

Four Effective Steps in Writing Counterarguments:

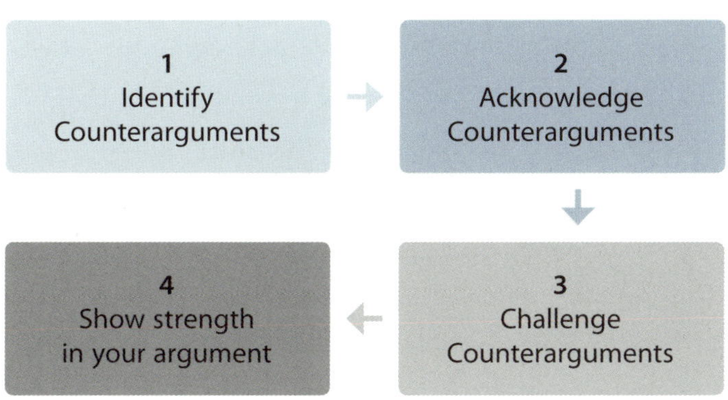

*Example*

| | |
|---|---|
| **Some may argue that the significant physical separation from the world's population hubs can be an inhibiting factor for the success of the tourist industry.** | **1. Identify counterarguments** |
| It is true that Australia is one of the most remote countries on Earth, and overseas travelers spend an average of 17 hours reaching Australia, a duration twice as long as the travel time to other geographically distinct destinations (Proctor & Thomas, 2014). | 2. Acknowledge counterarguments |
| *However, it may not negatively impact tourist numbers as much as initially considered due to the opportunity for visitors to explore various unique geographic features in one trip within a safe cultural context. While Australia may receive fewer total visitors, each tourist tends to spend three times more time compared to the average duration spent in a single country, excluding the USA (DRET, 2020). The country compensates the physical obstacle by encouraging visitors to allocate more of their vacation budget for a distinctive experience.* | *3. Challenge counterarguments* |
| **Consequently, Australia remains a premier destination that offers unparalleled and unforgettable adventures despite its geographical challenges.** | **4. Show strength in your argument** |

## B. Expressing Limitations

When composing a concluding paragraph, acknowledging the limitations of the essay is not considered a weakness of the writer's own research, but demonstrates a comprehensive understanding of the scope of the research.

*Example*

In conclusion, Australia's immense appeal to tourists arises from its unparalleled geological features and diverse wildlife. **While the nation benefits substantially from the tourism sector, the challenges of the geographic distance from major global hubs were not discussed in this essay. Also, the research was limited to the years 2010 to 2014, and a broader timeframe may offer varied insights.** Future research could examine evolving tourist preferences, especially in the post-pandemic era, and assess the potential impact of virtual tourism. Ultimately, despite its remoteness, Australia's ability to provide a unique, consolidated experience ensures tourists find the journey worth their time and resources.

## 3.3. Incorporating Tables and Figures

Effective use of tables and figures improves clarity and helps the reader understand complex data more easily. Selecting appropriate types of tables and figures enhances the effectiveness of your evidence.

### A. Formatting Tables and Figures

When integrating tables and figures, follow the guidelines below.

- Separate them from the text.
- Center them on the page.
- Assign table or figure number in the order they have appeared in the essay.
- Include the source of the data.

***Example***

**Table 1.** Shares of Energy-Related Emissions of Carbon Dioxide (Economic Sector in United States, 2021)

| Total | 4.6 Billion Metric Tons |
|---|---|
| Transportation | 38% |
| Electric Power | 33% |
| Industrial | 17% |
| Residential | 7% |
| Commercial | 5% |

## B. Describing Tables and Figures

Describing tables or figures is crucial to demonstrate the relevance of them to the arguments. Introduce the tables and figures by number (e.g., Table 1, Figure 2, etc.) and highlight key elements that support your points.

***Example***

Figure 2 displays the unemployment rates in several countries in the Asia-Pacific region for the year 2021. As demonstrated in the figure, China has the highest unemployment rate at 4.82%. This is likely due to the multiple lockdowns imposed during the COVID-19 pandemic.

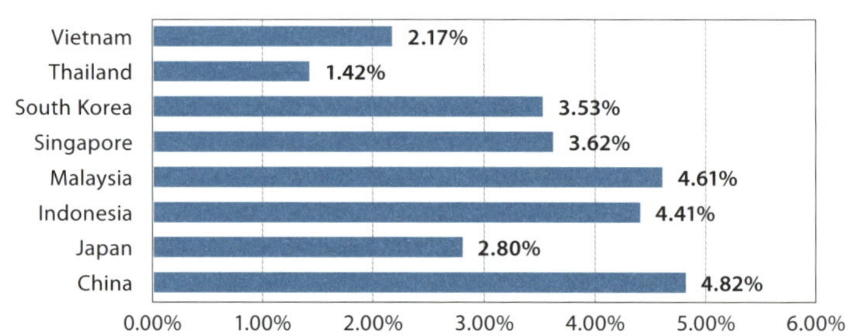


**Figure 2.** Unemployment rates in the Asia-Pacific region in 2021 (Statista 2023)

## 3.4. Citations and Referencing

### A. In-text Citation

When integrating sources into an essay, the writer must decide whether to emphasize **information** or **authorship**. These styles vary by academic field and the extent of the source's contribution. Information prominence ensures data accuracy and transparency, while authorship prominence focuses on the history of ideas in a field. By using both styles, academic writing can meet the specific requirements of different study fields and encourage clear communication and scholarly discussions.

#### a. Information Prominence

When the writer wants to emphasize the information they are presenting, they place the information at the beginning of the sentence and provide the source citation at the end. This style is particularly beneficial when the cited information is more important than the author. It is commonly used in the field of STEM to present information more objectively.

#### b. Author Prominence

This approach is used when the credibility and expertise of the author are important. Author prominent citations highlight the author's name at the beginning of a sentence to emphasize the author's contribution to the work. This style is commonly used in the fields of Humanities and Social Sciences because many of the sources a writer uses often include personal opinions.

***Examples***

**APA**:

- One way in which toddlers can develop their critical thinking skills is through storytelling with their caregivers **(Smith, 2010)**.
- **Smith (2010)** points out the importance of storytelling with toddlers as a tool for developing their critical thinking skills.

**MLA**:

- In a recent study, patients exposed to a high level of stress demonstrated a much quicker reduction in stress levels when given a cat to hold than those without a cat **(Brooks 32)**.
- **Brooks (32)** found that after being put in high-stress situations, participants who were given a cat to hold were able to reduce their stress five times more quickly than participants who were not given a cat.

**IEEE**:

- Several recent studies **[3, 4, 16]** have suggested that foreign-affiliated businesses in Japan tend to create more jobs than domestic ones, and that they tend to have higher productivity.
- According to research company Coherent Market Insights' forecast, the present $33 billion digital image market will grow by about $15 billion by 2028 [3].

### B. End-text Citations: Reference List

Writers should include a separate reference list at the end of their paper. This not only helps readers in finding the sources but also ensures that all cited materials are properly acknowledged.

There are various referencing styles depending on the field of study. For example, APA is most commonly used in education, psychology and the sciences, while MLA is more often used in the Humanities. Engineering majors and related fields commonly utilize IEEE style.

## Academic Journal Article

**APA:**

Sanguesa, J. A., Torres-Sanz, V., Garrido, P., Martinez, F. J., & Marquez-Barja, J. M. (2021). A review on electric vehicles: Technologies and challenges. *Smart Cities, 4*(1), 372-404. https://doi.org/10.3390/smartcities4010022

**MLA:**

Sanguesa, Julio A., et al. "A Review on Electric Vehicles: Technologies and Challenges." *Smart Cities*, vol. 4, no. 1, 2021, pp. 372-404. https://doi.org/10.3390/smartcities4010022.

**IEEE:**

[1] J. A. Sanguesa, V. Torres-Sanz, P. Garrido, F. J. Martinez, and J. M. Marquez-Barja, "A review on electric vehicles: Technologies and challenges," *Smart Cities*, vol. 4, no. 1, pp. 372-404, 2021. [Online]. Available: https://doi.org/10.3390/smartcities4010022. [Accessed Mar 30, 2023]

## Websites

**APA:**

United Nations Environment Programme. (2022, February 06). *Annual Report 2022*. UNEP. https://www.unep.org/resources/annual-report-2022

**MLA:**

"Annual Report 2022." *UNEP - UN Environment Programme*, www.unep.org/resources/annual-report-2022.

**IEEE:**

[1] "Annual Report 2022," *UNEP*, February 06, 2022. [Online]. Available: https://www.unep.org/resources/annual-report-2022. Accessed on: Feb. 6, 2022. [Accessed Mar 30, 2023]

## Book

**APA:**

Nakajima, T., Hamori, S., He, X., Liu, G., Zhang, W., Zhang, Y., & Liu, T. (2021). *ESG investment in the global economy*. Springer Nature.

**MLA:**

Nakajima, Tadahiro, et al. *ESG Investment in the Global Economy*. Springer, 2021.

**IEEE:**

[1] T. Nakajima, S. Hamori, X. He, G. Liu, W. Zhang, Y. Zhang, & T. Liu. *ESG Investment in the Global Economy*. Springer, 2021.

## eBook

**APA:**

Barry, J. R., Lee, E. A., & Messerschmitt, D. G. (2004). *Digital Communication*. Springer Science & Business Media. https://doi.org/10.1007/987-1-4615-0227-2

**MLA:**

Barry, J. R., Lee, E. A., and Messerschmitt, D. G. *Digital Communication*. Springer Science & Business Media, https://doi.org/10.1007/987-1-4615-0227-2.

**IEEE:**

[1] J. R. Barry, E. A. Lee, and D. G. Messerschmitt, *Digital Communication*, Springer Science & Business Media, 2004. [E-book]. Available: https://doi.org/10.1007/987-1-4615-0227-2.

**Table 2.4.** Websites for referencing

| **American Psychological Association (APA)** |
| --- |
| https://apastyle.apa.org/ → click 'STYLE AND GRAMMAR GUIDELINES' |
| **Modern Language Association (MLA) guide center** |
| https://style.mla.org/ → click 'Citing Sources' → 'Citations by Format' |
| **Institute of Electrical and Electronics Engineers (IEEE) author center** |
| Click 'https://journals.ieeeauthorcenter.ieee.org/create-your-ieee-journal-article/create-the-text-of-your-article/ieee-editorial-style-manual/,' find the file 'IEEE Reference Guide. |

# 4. Coherence and Cohesion

In an academic essay, **coherence** refers to the logical flow and organization of ideas. It involves their smooth and logical progression. Each sentence or paragraph should build upon the preceding one. **Cohesion** relates to the grammatical and lexical linking within a text or sentence that hold a text together and give it meaning. It commonly involves the use of connective words, pronouns, and conjunctions to link sentences and paragraphs. Below are some common strategies to enhance coherence and cohesion of an essay.

## 4.1. Transition Signals

**Transition signals** are linguistic tools that connect ideas and guide readers through a text, enhancing its flow and clarity. They can indicate addition, contrast, cause and effect, or sequence. These signals can be placed at the beginning or within sentences to illustrate relationships between points.

Effective use of transition signals improves comprehensibility of written content.

***Example***

There are two economic burdens on singles today. The first burden is the high cost of living. For instance, payments for electricity are increasing, and the prices for vegetables and fruits are skyrocketing. As a result, it has become extremely difficult to afford living expenses and have any remaining funds for personal pleasure. The second financial obstacle is the high cost of housing. Many young people save money in order to purchase a house, but saving money is not easy. In fact, studies indicate that it usually takes 30 years to accumulate enough funds to buy a house, even if one refrains from spending their wages entirely. Consequently, if this situation continues, the younger generation will refuse to marry and have a family.

### A. Transition signals: Chronological order

When describing a sequence of steps, ideas, or a process in an academic essay, using transition signals that express chronological order is highly recommended. They make the essay clearer and more logical for readers to follow.

| |
|---|
| First, Firstly, To begin with, First of all, |
| **Second, Secondly, The second (reason) is..., ... is the second (reason), The next (reason) is...** |
| **Finally, Last but not least, The last (reason) is...** |

*Examples*

**First of all**, the government should gather information from the companies that are related to the incidence. The reason is...

**Finally**, the government should reinforce the regulations that were established by...

### B. Transition Signals: Examples

For example, As an example, For instance, To illustrate, To demonstrate

*Examples*

**For instance**, the global influence of K-culture can be examined by the widespread popularity of K-pop music and Korean dramas across diverse international audiences.

**To illustrate**, leadership styles vary across different contexts, emphasizing autocratic decision-making, democratic collaboration, or laissez-faire delegation.

### C. Transition Signals: To Add More Information

**In addition, Additionally, Furthermore, Moreover**

*Examples*

**In addition**, incorporating regular exercise into one's routine not only improves physical health but also enhances mental well-being.

**Moreover**, diversity in the workplace brings together individuals with varied perspectives, experiences, and skills, leading to enhanced. creativity and innovation.

### D. Transition Signals: Compare and Contrast

**In contrast, however, on the other hand, on the contrary, alternatively, unlike, nevertheless, whereas, similarly, likewise, in the same way, just as, as with, equally, in a similar fashion, accordingly**

*Examples*

Having an electric charger attached to the device itself is advantageous. **On the other hand**, it can be quite inconvenient because it may be very heavy.

**Alternatively**, organizations can implement flexible work arrangements, such as telecommuting or compressed workweeks, to enhance employee work-life balance.

**NOTE**

Certain transition signals can be used in different locations within a sentence.

**Unlike** the bustling city center, the quiet suburbs provide a serene atmosphere.

In terms of climate, the tropical region is hot and humid year-round, **unlike** the temperate zone which experiences distinct seasons.

## E. Transition Signals: Results

**Therefore, Thus, Hence, As a result, As a consequence, Consequently**

*Examples*

**Therefore**, considering the potential risks and benefits, it is imperative to conduct thorough risk assessments before implementing new technologies.

**Consequently**, the economic performance of any company depends on the quality of its staff.

## F. Transition Signals: Conclusion

**In summary, To summarize, To sum up, To conclude, In conclusion, In summary, In short, Finally, Overall, Thus, Therefore, Hence, All in all**

*Examples*

**To sum up**, the history of women's voting rights in Europe is divided into three distinct time periods.

**To conclude**, the two primary causes of obesity are excess calories and insufficient exercise.

## 4.2. Synonyms

Using **synonyms** is another effective way to increase coherence. Developing paragraphs with a variety of academic vocabulary ensures a stronger and more engaging piece of writing. Repeated use of the same words can weaken an essay's strength, and use of synonyms is one way to avoid repetition.

- Use a **thesaurus** to search for synonyms. It is available in online dictionaries.

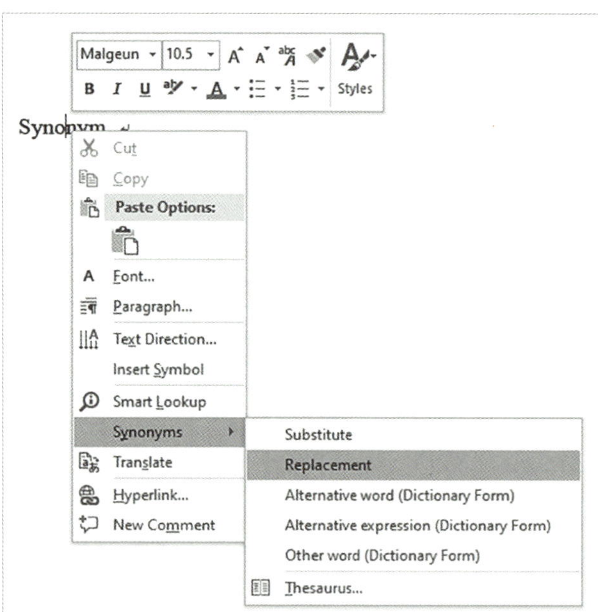


- Use the **synonym** function in MS Word to see available suggestions.

- Make sure the **meaning** remains unchanged when replacing a word.

Compare paragraphs A and B below.

[A] Paragraph containing repeated words

As more people move to cities, more people will need to seek work and places to live. As the population increases, the demand for work and places to live will increase. As the demand increases, the quality of life in general, will decrease, and there will be an increase in problems in society.

[B] Paragraph modified with synonyms

As more people move to cities, **those citizens** will need to seek **jobs** and places to live. **Once** the population increases, the demand for work and **houses** will also **rise**. As the demand **escalates**, the quality of life in general will decrease and there will be an increase in problems in society.

**TASK**

Read the following paragraph and replace the repeated words with synonyms.

*One of the main problems with an electric car is the fire problem. As the use of electric cars increases, the number of electric cars that catch fire increases. One of the most frequent times that a fire occurs is when an electric car is charged. However, the more problematic issue with an electric car is a battery problem.*

## 4.3. Reference Words

**Reference words** are terms used to refer back to information stated earlier without repeating the same words or phrases. They help to connect ideas and sentences more tightly.

### A. Pronouns

Use pronouns as reference words when the noun they are replacing is clear. Make sure this noun is close by, ideally in the previous sentence.

***Example***

> When purchasing an item, people consider price, quality, design, trend, and functionality. **They** are all important factors in decision making.

> To bring a sustainable future for the economy, companies must incorporate environment, society, and government (ESG) in their policies. If **they** are well established and practiced in companies…

### B. Summary Words

Summary words are another type of reference words, designed to summarize previously mentioned ideas into a single term or phrase.

***Examples***

> For example, the favorite destinations included Uluru, beaches, and tropical rainforests. Uluru is the world's largest rock structure (DRET, 2015). **This formation** is so rare that the Uluru-Kata Tjuta National Park is one of the few World Heritage properties listed for both its natural and cultural values (Georgiou, 2017, p. 21).

Smith (2023) and Franks (2021) state that hydrogen energy is the best alternative energy source in the future. **This** research clearly demonstrates the importance of future energy development.

Secondly, houses are often overcrowded and have poor air circulation. Not only that, the number of residents in one household is 3 times higher than an average household according to the government census (Bradford, 2011). **Such conditions** make it easier for the residents to catch diseases like the flu, TB, and diphtheria, where infection enters through the throat (Smith, 2010).

Additionally, it is already known that B.t. toxins cause death in many species of insect larvae (Verma et al., 2011). Despite the importance of **this knowledge**, there is a lack of studies in this area.

# 5. Academic Language

**Academic language** refers to specific language and writing style used in academic contexts. Academic language differs from conversational language in terms of its formality, precision, and adherence to established standards. Developing academic language skills is important because it not only helps to convey ideas and information clearly, but serves as a sign of professionalism. Academic language provides a common ground for communication across various academic disciplines and using it ensures that your work can be understood by others in your discipline and beyond.

## 5.1. Academic Vocabulary

Academic vocabulary refers to the specialized language and terminology that is commonly used in academic and scholarly contexts. When writing an academic paper, it is important to use formal words and phrases that are different from informal words that are used in everyday (colloquial) conversation such as: things, stuff, like, kids, and guys. Using appropriate academic vocabulary is essential as it helps to establish disciplinary identity and enhances the clarity of communication. Scholars have classified words into three categories: **general words**, **academic words**, and **technical words**.

### A. General Words

General words are words that are used in everyday life but are still acceptable to be used in academic writing as they form the **'core'** of the English language. West (1953) identified over 2,000 words as the General Service List (GSL) and an updated list of 2,818 words was created in 2013 by Browne, Culligan, and Phillips.

### B. Academic Words

Academic words are words that are commonly used in academic writing, research, and formal communication within educational contexts. These words are often more complex and specific than general words, and are used in various academic disciplines to communicate ideas accurately. The New Academic Word List (Browne, Culligan, & Phillips, 2013) includes a list of 963 words, and some examples of academic words are: **analyze**, **approach**, **assess**, **derive**, **evaluate**, **hypothesis**, **interpret**, **methodology**, and **significant**.
Please compare the two sentences below in terms of formality.

- Colloquial: "There are **some things** we can do to relax, **like** taking a walk or meditating."

- Academic: "There are **many ways** to relax, **such as** taking a walk or meditating."

*** For more academic words, see site at EAP Foundation**
(https://www.eapfoundation.com/vocab/academic/awllists/)

### C. Technical Words

Technical words are the terms that are used within certain disciplines. When writing an academic paper in the field of Engineering, the terms used are going to be different to those used in Biology or Sociology. Therefore, it is necessary to provide definitions of certain technical terminology, as the particular field addressed in the writing may be new to the reader.

- Hypothesis (Scientific research)
- Regression analysis (Statistics)
- Paradigm (Social sciences)
- Algorithm (Computer science)
- Mitosis (Biology)
- Hegemony (Sociology)

**TASK**

Think about your own major. What are some technical terms that are unique to your field of study?

**NOTE**

#### Useful websites to enhance vocabulary

| | |
|---|---|
| Thesaurus | www.thesaurus.com |
| Online dictionaries | https://dictionary.cambridge.org/<br>https://www.oxfordlearnersdictionaries.com/<br>https://www.ldoceonline.com/ |
| Collocations | https://flax.nzdl.org/greenstone3/<br>flax?a=fp&sa=collAbout&c=collocations |
| Corpus of Contemporary American English | https://www.english-corpora.org/coca/ |

## 5.2. Balancing Objectivity and Subjectivity

Understanding the difference between objective and subjective language is important in academic writing. Objective language is characterized by a neutral tone, while subjective language often conveys personal opinions or perspectives using first-person pronouns. Understanding the distinction between objective and subjective language allows writers to communicate effectively and maintain credibility in academic writing. While academic writing typically requires objectivity and evidence-based arguments, certain writing types such as critique, editorials, or opinion columns in newspapers involve subjective language.

### A. Objective Language

Objective language is used when describing facts and research that has come to a clear conclusion. The primary purpose is presenting facts, evidence, and information in a clear and unbiased manner.

***Example***

> Figure 1 **shows** that chatbots ensure quick responses and customer satisfaction.
> The results of this study **revealed** a statistically significant correlation between groups A and B.

### B. Subjective Language

Subjective language is employed in academic writing to convey personal opinions and interpretations. It includes words or phrases that show personal viewpoints, emotions, inferences, guesses, or evaluations, instead of an objective presentation of proven facts or neutral descriptions. It often has words that suggest possibility (e.g., might, could), adjectives that express opinions (e.g., wonderful, poor), and adverbs that change how strong a statement is (e.g., really, very).

*Example*

> A 2017 study on the brains of deceased American Football players revealed that 99% exhibited signs of Chronic Traumatic Encephalopathy (CTE). Therefore, preventative action **must** be taken now to protect the players' health.

### C. Reporting Verbs

Reporting verbs introduce information, opinions, or ideas of someone else in academic writing. They allow writers to refer to sources or other texts, conveying the nature of the information or the stance the original author might have taken. Reporting verbs are crucial for distinguishing between the writer's perspective and that of the sources being cited.

**Table 2.4.** Reporting Verbs

| Verb Type | Weaker Position | Neutral Position | Stronger Position |
|---|---|---|---|
| Agreeing | Acknowledge | Agree | Concur |
| | Admit | Confirm | Support |
| | Recognize | Validate | Embrace |
| | Accept | Affirm | Endorse |
| | Concede | Corroborate | Advocate |
| Disagreeing | Disapprove | Disagree | Reject |
| | Disagree | Contradict | Refute |
| | Object | Counter | Challenge |
| | Oppose | Contend | Dismiss |
| | Deny | Dispute | Disavow |
| | | | Strongly oppose |
| Explaining | Clarify | Explain | Elaborate |
| | Describe | Present | Expound |
| | Outline | Illustrate | Demonstrate |
| | Define | Indicate | Emphasize |
| | Provide | Note | Highlight |
| | | Point out | Substantiate |

*Examples*

**Agreeing**:

1. Weaker Position: "The report **acknowledges** the validity of this hypothesis in existing literature."
2. Neutral Position: "Scholars **confirm** that the findings align with established research in the field."
3. Stronger Position: "Numerous studies **concur** with the proposed theoretical framework."

**Disagreeing**:

1. Weaker Position: "They **object to** the methodology used in this analysis within the academic community."
2. Neutral Position: "Researchers respectfully **disagree with** the interpretation of the statistical data."
3. Stronger Position: "Prominent scholars **strongly oppose** the assertion due to substantial methodological limitations."

**Explaining**:

1. Weaker Position: "The group briefly **clarified** the fundamental concepts underpinning this theoretical framework."
2. Neutral Position: "This section aims to **explain** the pivotal factors contributing to the success of the project."
3. Stronger Position: "The following section will **elaborate** on the intricate details that constitute the foundation of this theory, providing a comprehensive understanding."

*Examples*

**Other Examples**

- State/Assert: She **states** that children learn best through play.
- Argue/Claim: Johnson **argues** that environmental regulations are insufficient.
- Suggest/Propose: The study **suggests** a correlation between diet and mental health.
- Believe/Think: Some scientists **believe** the phenomenon is due to climate change.

For more, see ***'Verbs for reporting verbs by University of Adelaide'*** (https://www.adelaide.edu.au/writingcentre/sites/default/files/docs/learningguide-verbsforreporting.pdf)

### D. Hedging

Hedging refers to using cautious or moderate language to express uncertainty, tentativeness, or the possibility of exceptions in making statements. It is a way to acknowledge the limitations of your research or the potential for alternative interpretations. In academic writing, hedging is important to take an objective approach and to demonstrate that you are open to different perspectives. However, overusing it can

**Table 2.5.** Hedging Language

| Category | Vocabulary |
|---|---|
| **Modal verbs** | may, might, can, could, will, would, should, ought to |
| **Verbs** | seem to, tend to, appear to, suggest, indicate, propose, recommend |
| **Adjectives** | possible, probable, likely, unlikely, doubtful, uncertain |
| **Adverbs** | possibly, probably, seemingly, approximately, generally, apparently, perhaps, maybe, presumably |
| **Nouns** | possibility, probability, likelihood, assumption, tendency, evidence, trend |

weaken your writing, so balancing is recommended to convey both confidence in your ideas and an understanding of the complexities within your field.

**TASK**

Look at the following pairs of sentences and discuss any differences in the meaning between the two.

- Young people these days do not want to marry and raise a family.
- It seems that many young people now are hesitant to marry and raise a family.

- The cost of living will continue to increase over the next ten years.
- There is a strong possibility that the cost of living may continue to increase over the next ten years.

- AI doctors cannot replace human doctors.
- It is not likely that AI doctors will replace human doctors.

## 5.3. Sentence Types

In academic writing, handling complex ideas requires the use of various sentence types. Different sentence structures facilitate clearer expression of thoughts. They also show that you can adapt your writing style to different contexts and communicate complex ideas effectively. There are four common sentence types: **simple**, **compound**, **complex**, and **compound-complex sentences**.

### A. Simple Sentence

A simple sentence consists of one independent clause.

*Example*

- Nuclear power plants are safer than commonly believed.
- One of the advantages of human doctors over A.I. is the ability to communicate with patients.
- Social media has become the primary form of communication for younger generations.

### B. Compound Sentence

A compound sentence is made up of two independent clauses (i.e., two simple sentences) with **a coordinating conjunction OR a semicolon**.

***Coordinating Conjunctions***: For, And, Nor, But, Or, Yet, So (FANBOYS)

*Examples*

The company released its first model. It became extremely popular in the market.

↓

The company released its first model, **and** it became extremely popular in the market.

↓

The company released its first model; it became extremely popular in the market.

**NOTE**

**DO NOT USE FANBOYS** at the beginning of a sentence.

Add a **comma** before a coordinating conjunction.

### C. Complex Sentence

A complex sentence contains an independent clause and a dependent clause connected with a subordinating conjunction (Table 2.5).

**Table 2.5.** Subordinating Conjunctions

| Type | Subordinators |
| --- | --- |
| **Time** | before, after, when, whenever, until, as soon as, while, since, as |
| **Contrast** | even though, although, though, whereas, while |
| **Cause & Effect** | since, because, as |
| **Condition** | if, unless, as long as |

***Examples***

This government-driven project may become successful **if** the budget is secured and the manpower is guaranteed.

↓

**If** the budget is secured and the manpower is guaranteed, this government-driven project may become successful.

**NOTE**

When writing a complex sentence, a comma is needed when a dependent clause comes at the beginning of the sentence.

***If** the budget is secured and the manpower is guaranteed**,** this government-driven project may become successful.*

### D. Compound Complex Sentence

A compound-complex sentence combines elements of both compound and complex sentences. It contains two independent clauses and one or more dependent clauses.

*Examples*

**While** the digital revolution has significantly transformed industries across the globe, traditional sectors like agriculture have been slower to adapt**, yet** they are now beginning to integrate technological advancements to improve efficiency and sustainability.

**As** the global temperature continues to rise, some nations are investing heavily in renewable energy sources**, but** others still rely predominantly on fossil fuels.

## E. Common Sentence Structure Mistakes

### a. Sentence Fragments

A sentence fragment refers to an incomplete sentence that lacks one or more essential components, typically a subject or a verb. It does not express a complete thought on its own.

*Examples*

**Incorrect**: I decided to have a break. Because I was tired.
**Correct**: I decided to have a break **because** I was tired.

**Incorrect**: Jumped over the fence.
**Correct**: **He** jumped over the fence.

**Incorrect**: In class today, we discussed how to improve independence in learning. Also how to develop autonomy.
**Correct**: In class today, we discussed how to improve independence in learning**, and** how to develop autonomy.

### b. Run-On Sentences

This occurs when two or more independent clauses (complete thoughts) are improperly joined without the necessary punctuation or conjunctions.

*Examples*

**Incorrect**: It was hot, we went swimming.
**Correct**: It was hot**, so** we went swimming

**Incorrect**: It was hot, therefore, we went swimming.
**Correct**: It was hot**;** therefore, we went swimming.

**Incorrect**: He did not sleep well last night; so, he fell asleep in class.
**Correct**: He did not sleep well last night**;** he fell asleep in class.
**Correct**: He did not sleep well last night**, so** he fell asleep in class.

## 5.4. Punctuation

In academic writing, there are different punctuation symbols, and they each serve a very specific purpose. See punctuation symbols commonly used below (Table 2.6).

**Table 2.6.** Punctuation symbols

| Name | Symbol | Purpose |
|---|---|---|
| **Capitalization** | | Always used to start a new sentence |
| **Period** | . | To mark the end of a sentence |
| **Comma** | , | To join two independent clauses with a coordinating conjunction |
| **Quotation Marks** | "….." | Used to show the reader that something is being directly copied from another source |

| Name | Symbol | Purpose |
|---|---|---|
| **Hyphen** | - | Used to pair compound words |
| **Parentheses** | (...) | Used when citing to denote the year of publication |
| **Semicolon** | ; | Used to join two main clauses that are related |
| **Abbreviations** | | "UN" for "United Nations"<br>"NASA" for "National Aeronautics and Space Administration"<br>When introducing an acronym in a paper, spell the full term with the acronym in parenthesis. From the second time, just use the acronym<br>e.g., The United Nations (UN) is an international organization. My friend works for UN. |

For more on punctuation, see ***'Punctuation: Effective Writing Practices Tutorial by NORTHERN ILLINOIS UNIVERSITY'*** (https://www.niu.edu/writingtutorial/punctuation/capitalization.shtml)

Chapter 3

# PRESENTATION

*"The success of your presentation will be judged not by the knowledge you send but by what the listener receives."*

*- Lilly Walters*

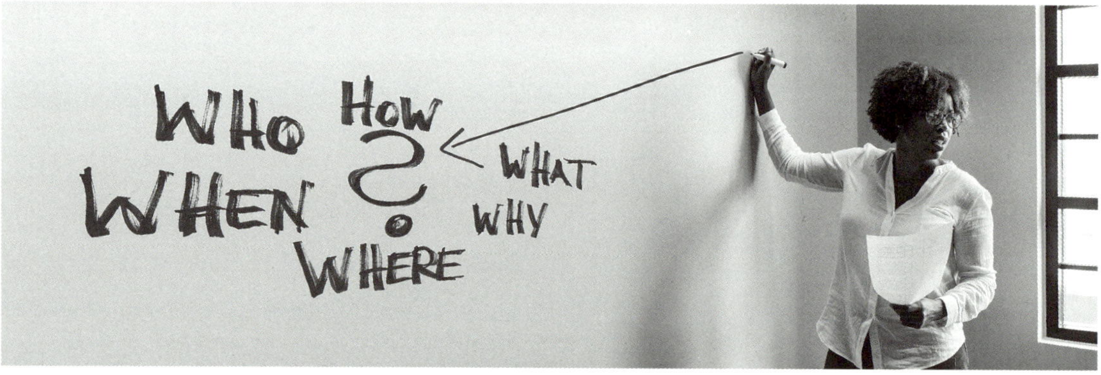

## 1. Introduction to Presentation

Creating a clear and engaging academic presentation is essential for sharing your ideas with the audience. This chapter will help you learn how to create and give presentations.

To give an effective presentation, preparation is important. Figure 3.1. illustrates the process of preparing for an academic presentation.

**Stage 1: Conceptualizing**

**Consider different ideas related to your topic.** Which ideas are related, and what do you want to include in your presentation?

**Stage 2: Researching**

**Look for key details and ideas for main points.** Make sure your information is credible and up-to-date.

**Stage 3: Outlining**

**Put together your ideas into the basic flow of a presentation.** Check your points are logical and your research supports them.

**Stage 4: Writing**

**Develop your outline more** – do this by making detailed notes, making cue cards and/or writing a full script.

**Stage 5: Revising**

**Review your work so far.** Do any parts feel awkward or disconnected? Do some parts need stronger evidence? No presentation is perfect; revising is improving!

**Stage 6: Practicing**

**Practice!** During this step you can (and usually do) make final changes, practice with cue cards, and carefully check that your visual aids flow well with what is said.

**Figure 3.1.** Preparing for an Academic Presentation: The Process

## 2. Presentation Structure

This section provides guidance on the basic structure of a presentation (Figure 3.2) with the detailed explanations of each section in an academic presentation.

| Introduction → | Body → | Conclusion |
|---|---|---|
| • Hook | • Main point 1 (MP1) | • Summary |
| • Greeting | • Main point 2 (MP2) | • Concluding remarks |
| • Focus statement | • Main point 3 (MP3) | |
| • Content preview | • … | |

**Figure 3.2.** Overall structure of an academic presentation

## Success of Australia's Tourism

| | |
|---|---|
| Have you ever travelled overseas this year? Is there anyone who has been to Europe? How about Australia? Anyone? Oh, Jenny, you have been to Australia. Which city did you visit? Sydney. Excellent. | **Introduction**<br>Hooks and introductory statements |
| Hello, my name is David majoring in business administration. | Greeting |
| Did you know that Australia's tourism industry contributes 3.2% to Australia's income according to Department of Foreign Affairs and Trade? Today, I am going to talk about why Australia's tourism is successful. The reason I chose this topic is because I was captivated by Australia's natural wonders and its booming tourism industry during my recent visit. | Focus statement |
| So, I am going to focus especially on the breathtaking landscapes, unique wildlife, and its economic impact. | Content preview |
| Are you ready? Let's begin. | Signpost |
| First, I would like to talk about Australia's unique geological and ecological features, which makes it a particularly attractive tourist location. According to a survey, close to 90% of tourist said a key reason to go to Australia is its extraordinary natural phenomena. What are they? The first location is Uluru. It is the world's largest stone. This formation is so rare that the Uluru-Kata Tjuta National Park is one of the few World Heritage properties listed for both its natural and cultural values. Another example is beaches. Australia has over 10,000 miles of white sandy beaches, some of the world's best surfing conditions. These two examples alone make me feel like I want to go to Australia and travel around. How about you? | **Body**<br>MP1 |
| Now, let's go deeper into the second captivating aspect that attracts numerous tourists from around the world to Australia. | Signpost |
| ......................... | MP2 |
| ......................... | MP3 |
| In conclusion, let's recap the key points covered in today's presentation. | **Conclusion**<br>Signpost |
| Australia's attraction lies in its stunning landscapes and distinct wildlife, and its remote location, which adds a sense of adventure and novelty for many travelers. | Summary |
| So, the next time you plan your trip, why don't you consider going to Australia? You won't be disappointed! Thank you. | Closing remarks |

## 2.1. Introduction

The introduction to a presentation holds great significance as it has the potential to captivate the audience with your message or completely lose them.

### A. Hooks

Catch your audience's attention right from the start with a strong opener to hook your audience. Here are **four** ideas on how to get started with your presentation: **Questions**, **Quotations**, **Facts and Statistics**, and **Narratives**.

#### a. Questions

Presenters can initiate audience participation through thought-provoking questions or by presenting a problem related to the topic. This approach serves as a simple yet effective method to actively engage the audience. However, it is crucial to ensure that the questions or problem(s) are genuinely intriguing and stimulate the audience's thinking process. As seen in the example below, some are **'rhetorical questions,'** which means that the audience is not expected to provide a response.

***Example***

> "How many hours a week do you work? Do you think it's too much? [pause] Did you know that among OECD countries, South Koreans work the fifth highest amount of hours per year?"

#### b. Quotations

Using a significant quote or proverb as the opening of a presentation can make it more compelling and impactful.

***Example***

> "Edward Deming, an American engineer famous for his management philosophy stated that: "94% of problems in business are systems driven and only 6% are people driven."

**c. Facts and Statistics**

Another approach is introducing a current surprising fact or statistic from a credible source. This technique can instantly grab the audience's attention and generate curiosity about the topic at hand.

***Example***

> "Did you know that the revenue of video streaming apps, such as Youtube, Netflix and Disney+, has more than doubled between 2018 and 2023? From $42.4billion dollars to $90.8billion dollars, according to this chart from Statista."

**d. Narratives: Personal Stories**

Utilizing narratives and anecdotes is an advanced yet highly impactful technique in presentations. Begin your presentation by sharing a personal experience that serves as a catalyst for discussing the topic.

***Example***

> "I'm usually very careful with my possessions, but once I accidentally left my cell phone on a table in a café. I panicked that it would be gone forever, but when I went back to the café, it was still there. Perhaps you've experienced this too – even in Korea's big cities, it is very rare that anyone would take your belongings."

### B. Greeting

The greeting is the part of the introduction where you briefly introduce yourself. The presenter should introduce themselves to the audience, but it is advisable not to spend too much time on this section. Keep it concise and focused to ensure that you have sufficient time for the main content of the presentation.

*"Hello, my name is ......... from the .... branch of ......"*
*"Good morning. I'm ...... from the department of ......"*

Try to link this to the **focus statement**:

*"... and today I will talk about..."*

### C. Focus Statement

A focus statement in an academic presentation is a clear and concise statement that introduces your topic and explains why you chose it.

***Example***

"Today, I will discuss the South Korean government's current efforts to address the declining birth rate because of **its significant impact on the nation's future**." 

Topic: South Korean government's current efforts to address the declining birth rate
Reason: its significant impact on the nation's future

### D. Content Preview

A content preview is a brief overview or roadmap of the main points of your presentation. By presenting the main points, you help the audience predict the key ideas.

*"I will introduce [*Main point 1 (MP1)*], then I will talk about [*Main point 2 (MP2)*], before explaining [*Main point 3 (MP3)*]."*
*"I'll discuss this topic in terms of 3 aspects: ..."*
*"The main points I will introduce today are ..."*

**TASK**

Identify the hook, greeting, and the focus statement. According to the content preview, what will the presenter do in this presentation?

*Imagine a world where artificial voices have become an integral part of our daily routines. From Siri's assistance to automated announcements during our commutes, synthetic speech has permeated our lives. However, amidst this progress, we must question whether there is still room for improvement or if we have reached a saturation point. Welcome, ladies and gentlemen. My name is Jisoo Kang, representing the computer science department. Today, I am excited to present my proposed topic for this semester: a critical analysis of the advancements in synthetic speech. My question is: Are these artificial voices truly as advanced as they can be? This will be answered through exploring three key areas: 1) the history and evolution of synthetic voices, 2) current applications and their effectiveness, and 3) potential areas of innovation and improvement for the future.*

## 2.2. Body

The body section plays a crucial role in an academic presentation, where a presenter explores the depths of the research and examines the main points. It offers a comprehensive analysis of evidence, examples, and data to enhance understanding of the topic and contribute to the existing knowledge. To achieve this, a few aspects should be considered.

The following is an example of how a presentation's main body points could be organized.

| | |
|---|---|
| **MP1: Breathtaking landscapes** | • Uluru: the world's largest stone<br>• 10,000 miles of white sandy beaches |
| **MP2: Unique wildlife** | • the Great Barrier Reef: the second most popular tourist destination in Australia<br>• Australian animals: kangaroos and koalas |
| **MP3: Economic impact** | • Stay 3 times longer than other countries<br>• As a result, spend more money in Australia |

## 2.3. Conclusion

The conclusion of a presentation provides the audience with the key 'takeaway' from your talk. To achieve this, it should include both a summary and closing remarks.

### A. Summary

The main points from the presentation should be summarized in the past tense to help the audience review the topic and understand the key points.

*"Today I explained [topic]. I told you about [MP1], explained how [MP2] was important, and finished by discussing [MP3]."*

*"In this presentation, I've analyzed [topic] and given three suggestions: [MP1, MP2, and MP3]."*

### B. Closing Remarks

Similar to the hook, closing remarks in an academic presentation aim to remind the audience of the presentation's purpose and create a lasting impression. One effective approach is to conclude with a thought-provoking question, a relevant statistic or quote, or a concise takeaway statement. These closing statements leave the audience with a specific message or idea to remember and reflect upon as they depart from the presentation.

There are **three** possible ways to end your presentation: **Restate the Importance of the Topic**, **Call to Action**, and **Mirror the hook**.

#### a. Restate the Importance of the Topic

Remind the audience why you wanted to present to them, why your topic is important, and why they should consider your contents in the future.

***Example***

> "Music is an important element of culture that touches people of all ages and from all backgrounds. Investment in music education now ensures that the culture continues to develop and thrive well into the future."

#### b. Call to Action

If you intend for your presentation to encourage people to change their habits, or act upon something, call upon them to do so at the end.

*Example*

"It is clear that the climate is changing, and that human behaviour is having an influence. We must make a choice: Change our lifestyle or embrace new methods to sustain it. That is why we must develop green energy solutions."

### c. Mirror the Hook

This technique involves revisiting the hook to emphasize its significance. This helps reinforce the main message and leaves a lasting impression on the audience.

*Examples*

**INTRODUCTION (Hook):**
"Speaking on the reasons to continue work in environmental conservation, broadcaster and naturalist Sir David Attenborough said "No one will protect what they don't care about, and no one will care about what they have never experienced."

**CONCLUDING REMARK (Mirroring the hook):**
"I'd like to end with another quote from Sir David Attenborough: "An understanding of the natural world is a source of not only great curiosity, but great fulfilment." We need to nurture the curiosity of the next generation to continue to care for our environment, to allow them the fulfilment that older generations have enjoyed."

# 3. Presentation Language

## 3.1. Signpost

In academic presentations, using 'signposts' between sections—such as transitioning from the introduction to MP1, from MP1 to MP2, and so forth until the conclusion—is crucial. Signposts help the audience digest the content and anticipate what is coming next. They not only maintain the audience's attention by outlining the structure of your talk but also enhance comprehension (Figure 3.3).

| Introduction (Introduction to MP1) | | |
|---|---|---|
| "Let's start with MP1" | "The first point I want to talk about is..." | "I'd like to begin by discussing..." |

↓

| Body | | |
|---|---|---|
| MP1: "First, let me start by telling you about [MP 1]." | MP2: "Now you know about [MP1], let me tell you about [MP2]." | MP3: "That was [MP2], now I'll explain [MP3]." |

↓

| Conclusion | | |
|---|---|---|
| "In conclusion..." | "To sum up..." | "To conclude..." |

**Figure 3.3.** Signposts in the introduction, body, and conclusion of an academic presentation

## 3.2. Formality

When preparing an academic presentation, you must consider the level of formality of your language. Choose appropriate words for the audience, context, and goals of your presentation (Table 3.2).

**Table 3.2.** Formality of language in an academic presentation

| | Formality: | Use: |
|---|---|---|
| Frozen/ Formal | Most | Situations of great respect and formal events |
| Semi-formal | | Spontaneous speech such as conversation |
| Casual | Least | Relaxed situations, friendly conversation |

*Examples*

**Frozen/Formal**

Good morning, everyone. Recent studies focusing on urban development and social dynamics have highlighted a concerning trend. When an area starts to decline, we witness an uptick in vandalism and crime. It's like a snowball effect; the worse the area becomes, the bigger the problems grow. But here's the silver lining: when we invest time and effort in taking care of an area, it's much easier to keep it in good shape.

**Semi-Formal**

Good morning, everyone. Recent studies have shown a worrying trend. When an area starts to go downhill, we start seeing more graffiti, damage, and crime. It's like a domino effect; the worse the area gets, the more issues we face. But the good news? When we put in the work to look after an area, it stays nice and is easier to manage.

**Casual**

Hello. So there's this study I came across. It basically says when a place starts looking shabby, things go downhill with more graffiti, broken windows, and crime. It's like, the worse it looks, the more problems pop up. But on the flip side, if we show a place some love and take care of it, it sticks around looking good for longer. Makes sense, right?

## 3.3. Written vs. Spoken Language

There are times when you need to present what you have written. To transform an essay into a presentation while keeping the main content, adjustments must be made due to different aspects of written and spoken languages (Table 3.3).

**Table 3.3.** Written and spoken languages

| Aspect | Essay (Written Language) | Presentation (Spoken Language) |
|---|---|---|
| Nature | Formal and detailed | Conversational and direct |
| Language Features | Complex sentences, advanced vocabulary, passive voice, thorough citations | Shorter sentences, active voice, rhetorical questions, repetition for emphasis, direct address to audience |
| Use of Contractions | Tends to avoid contractions for formality (e.g., "cannot" instead of "can't") | Frequent use of contractions for a natural, conversational tone (e.g., "can't", "won't", "I'm") |
| Transitions for Organization | Uses transition words and phrases for flow and connection (e.g., "furthermore", "however", "in addition") | Frequent use of direct signposting language (e.g., "moving on", "next", "let's turn to") |
| Audience Engagement | Relies on compelling writing and logical flow | Requires a combination of verbal cues, body language, visual aids, and direct audience interaction for clarity |

*Example*

**Written**

Many successful industries contribute to the GDP of Australia. One such industry, the tourism industry, contributes 3.2 per cent to Australia's income and is responsible for employing 4.9 per cent of the population (Department of Foreign Affairs and Trade, 2018). Australia, a land of contrasts and wonders, has consistently been a magnet for travelers worldwide. From the iconic Sydney Opera House and the Great Barrier Reef to the mysteries of the Outback, the country offers a range of attractions that few places can match. While its popularity among tourists is undeniable, pinpointing the exact reasons for this appeal requires a closer look. The success of Australia's tourism can be attributed to breathtaking landscapes, unique wildlife, and its economic impact.

**Spoken**

How many people here have travelled overseas this year? Is there anyone who has been to Europe? How about Australia? Anyone? Oh, Jenny, you have been to Australia. Which city did you visit? Sydney. Excellent. Hello my name is David majoring in Tourism. Did you know that Australia's tourism industry contributes 3.2 per cent to Australia's income and is responsible for employing according to Department of Foreign Affairs and Trade? Today, I am going to talk about why Australia's tourism is successful. The reason I chose this topic is because I was captivated by Australia's natural wonders during my recent visit and its booming tourism industry. So, I'll be focusing on a few exciting aspects – the breathtaking landscapes, the unique wildlife, and how all of this impacts the economy. Are you ready? Let's begin.

## 4. Delivery

Public speaking is an essential skill in various aspects of life, from university to professional settings. While a written paper demonstrates an author's arguments and analysis, a presentation serves as a platform to persuade the audience of the value and significance of the presenter's findings or opinions. The act of presenting encompasses both verbal and non-verbal elements of communication (Figure 3.4).

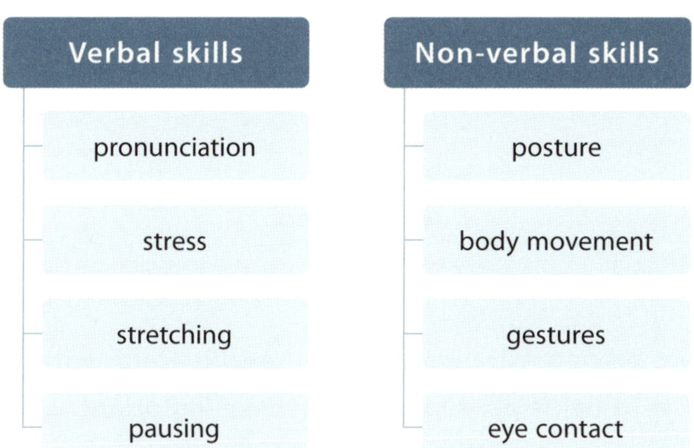


**Figure 3.4.** Verbal and Non-verbal delivery skills

## 4.1. Verbal Delivery Skills

In academic presentations, verbal language skills are crucial for conveying complex ideas and arguments effectively. These skills include **pronunciation**, **stress**, **stretching**, and **pausing**, all of which contribute to the overall quality and persuasiveness of the presentation. Through these verbal elements, presenters can better engage their audience and make their arguments more compelling. They are simple yet powerful tools that can help communicate more effectively and leave a strong impression on the audience.

### A. Pronunciation

While the primary goal of an academic presentation is clear message delivery, mispronunciations can lead to communication difficulties. For effective delivery of the message, clear pronunciation is necessary. One specific area that requires attention is the ability to distinguish between minimal pairs.

#### Minimal pairs

A minimal pair is a pair of words that differ in only one sound, usually a single consonant or vowel. For example, in English, the words "pat" and "bat" are minimal pairs because they differ in only one sound: the initial consonant sound, /p/ in "pat" and /b/ in "bat." The difference in this single sound changes the meaning of the two words.

Here are some more examples of minimal pairs in English:

| | |
|---|---|
| **p**an / **f**an | p**e**n / p**a**n |
| **b**oat / **v**ote | b**i**t / b**ea**t |
| b**l**ue / b**r**ew | sh**i**p / sh**ee**p |

### B. Stress

Stress involves placing extra emphasis on specific words within your sentences. It helps you highlight the most important words. By using stress, you can make your presentation more engaging and comprehensible.

TASK

Try these sentences with stress on different words and see how altering the stress changes the meaning.

1. **You** want me to give you money?
2. You want **me** to give you money?
3. You want me to **give** you money?
4. You want me to give **you** money?
5. You want me to give you **money**?

### C. Stretching

Stretching involves extending specific sounds within words. This technique is similar to adding a musical touch to your speech. When applied appropriately, stretching can improve the presentation's flow and engage the audience.
For instance, stretching can be used to express excitement or surprise more vividly:

*"Wow, it's sooooooo good!"*
*"That's amaaazing!"*
*"I can't belieeeve it!"*

### D. Pausing

A pause means taking short breaks between sentences or ideas. Pausing gives your audience time to think and understand what you said. However, long and frequent pauses can disrupt the flow of your speech. Well-timed pauses will allow the audience to process what has been said without losing interest.

*"The winner is... **[pause]** John!"*
*"As she opened the mysterious box… **[pause]** she couldn't believe what she found inside!... **[pause]** It was the most incredible surprise."*

**TASK**

Practice the following sentences, which describe a coffee shop, using the techniques of stress, stretching, and pause. Refer to the technique labels in the box.

*This place is <-lively->* ***but*** *has a <-relaxing-> (...) atmosphere.*
*There are <-many-> chairs (...) and tables.*
*There is a* ***great*** *(...) view from a <-long-> window.*

| Technique Labels |
|---|
| **Stress** |
| <-Stretch-> |
| Pause (...) |

The use of the techniques can serve to highlight key information or keep the audience engaged during your presentation.

**NOTE**

## Fillers

In everyday conversation, people often use fillers, such as "ummm" and "errrr" as they think and speak at the same time. In presenting, this usually happens when someone is nervous or unprepared. For example:

*"Let me,* ***err****, start by giving some of the,* ***ummm****, background of this topic. As I said,* ***erm****, we* ***err****, often hear synthetic,* ***erm****, voices in our* ***ummm*** *everyday lives."*
Using too many fillers will disrupt the flow of the presentation, and give the impression that the speaker lacks confidence.

### Ways to reduce the use of fillers

1. Record your presentation.
2. Count how often fillers occur in your speech.
3. Find the parts where you commonly use these fillers.
4. When tempted to use a filler, take a pause to give yourself a moment to collect your thoughts and continue with clarity.

## 4.2. Non-verbal Delivery Skills

Non-verbal communication complements verbal communication, enhancing the connection with the audience. This section will introduce four non-verbal delivery skills for an effective presentation: **posture**, **body movement**, **gestures**, and **eye contact**.

> *"The most important thing in communication is to hear what is not said."*
>
> *- Peter Drucker*

### A. Posture

Posture refers to the way you hold your body when standing or sitting. In the context of presentations, posture involves how you stand and face your audience. It is widely considered to be a significant indicator of a presenter's confidence. Since the audience's initial impression is often formed based on the presenter's posture, establishing a favorable first impression is crucial.

### Examples of Posture

Good posture will naturally vary from person to person. Below are some tips as to what a presenter can do to 'look good' to the audience, and what they should avoid doing.

Always face your audience. Don't turn your body towards your visuals or turn your back on the audience.

Don't 'slouch' – it can make you appear lazy and uninterested in your own speech! Stand tall and confident.

Try not to stand too stiffly. It can make you look uncomfortable and come across as too formal to your audience.

If you are holding cue cards, keep them around waist-height. Hold them in one hand so you can gesture freely.

### B. Body Movement

In academic presentations, effective body movement serves as more than just a visual aid; a confident presenter often moves while they present, shifting the focus of their eye contact. The way a presenter moves can emphasize important points, guide transitions between topics, and maintain audience interest. That is, effective body movement contributes to clearer communication and greater audience engagement.

#### Exercise

Place some Xs on the floor and use them to practice your presentation. Begin from the central X and engage your audience with the first lines of your presentation. After that, move to the second X and continue presenting. After a brief moment, move to the final X, and repeat. Always keep your feet facing the audience and avoid turning your back on them when you walk around.

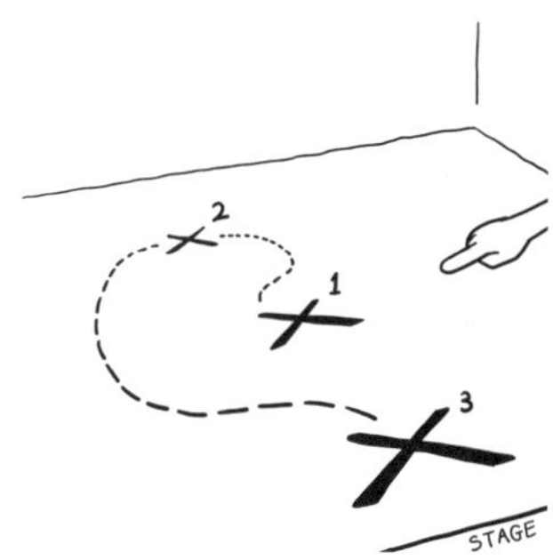


### C. Gestures

> "As the tongue speaketh to the ear, so the gesture speaketh to the eye"
>
> \- Sir Francis Bacon

We cannot communicate effectively with our voices alone. "Gestures are a vital part of speech and essential for delivering the message effectively in a presentation." A gesture involves moving one or both hands from a resting position, and then returning them. **Natural gestures** arise spontaneously during speech and are not rehearsed. They are a natural extension of the speaker's thought process and emotions. Natural gestures can make a speaker appear more genuine and passionate about their topic.

Another type of gestures are **pre-planned gestures**. These gestures are deliberately thought out and practiced before the presentation. A speaker might decide in advance to use a specific gesture to emphasize a particular point. Pre-planned gestures often align very closely with the content being presented. For instance, a speaker might spread their arms wide when discussing "expanding opportunities" or point upwards when referencing growth.

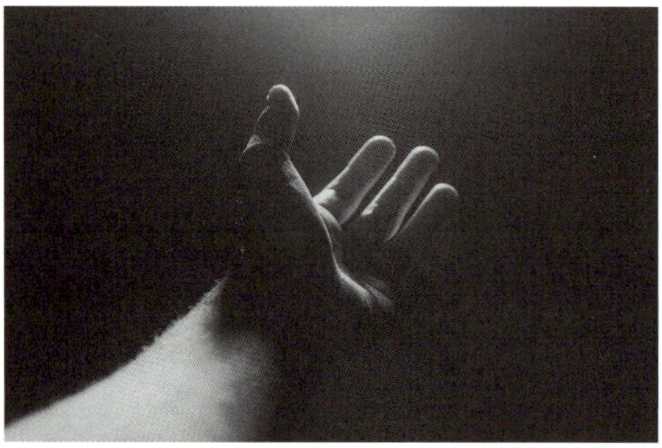

NOTE

## Cultural Relativity

Using certain gestures can create problems depending on cultural contexts and specific situations. When meeting people from different cultures, we need to be conscious of gestures as they may carry different meanings, or even cause offense. Consider some common gestures in your own culture. Would they be understood if you used them in a presentation? Do they have different meanings in other cultures?

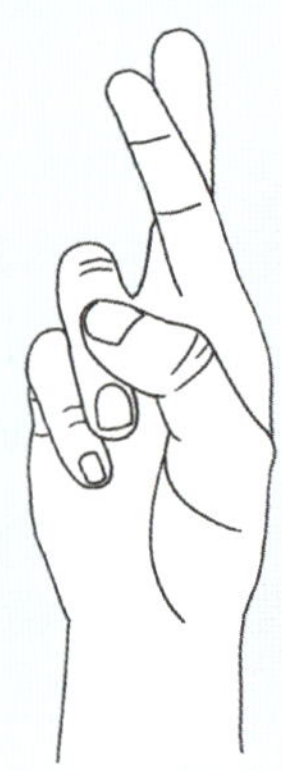

For instance, the "Fingers Crossed" gesture has a variety of meanings, but it is most commonly associated with the idea of protection (Morris et al., 1979). However, it is fairly common in some parts of South-East Europe to mean breaking a friendship. Therefore, displaying such a gesture in different parts of Europe could create different reactions from the audience.

### D. Eye Contact

Eye contact in academic presentations helps establish a connection with the audience, making the material more engaging. It also enhances the presenter's credibility by conveying confidence and sincerity. Additionally, maintaining eye contact allows the presenter to track the audience's reactions, and enable real-time adjustments.

#### Eye contact for different audience sizes

Presenters will face different audience sizes. When presenting to a large audience, it is difficult to make eye contact with everyone. To include everyone, divide the audience into three sections (left, middle, and right), and try to make direct eye contact with people in each section. Remember to make eye contact with an audience member for 2-3 seconds before moving to another section.

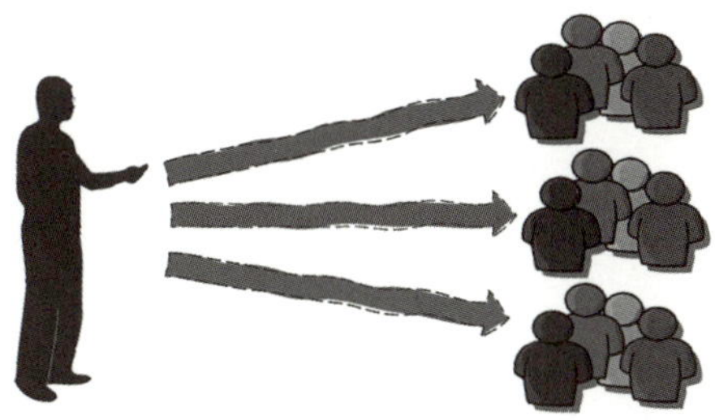

---

**TIP** **Audience Behavior**

Do you have any responsibility as an audience member? A good audience member is crucial for making a presentation successful and enjoyable for both the speaker and the listeners. Here are some tips on how to be a good audience member.

- Listen attentively
- Nod to indicate understanding
- Smile to show encouragement
- Applaud to express appreciation
- Avoid side conversations
- Ask thoughtful questions
- Provide feedback

## 4.3. Video Presentation

Video presenting has become a feature of academic conferences in recent years. This could take the form of a pre-recorded video or a live presentation through the medium of streaming software. Presenting in this way retains the same structural and visual presentation elements; however, some elements of physical delivery change. This section will review some of the key features of presenting through digital media.

### A. Considerations When Recording

- Make sure to check your camera and computer equipment thoroughly. Use a high quality camera, check the audio, and practice with your visual aids. Test all of these carefully before presenting.
- Video presentations will typically be made while seated. Therefore, consider the position of the camera. It should be not too close or too far from you, and would ideally be at eye level.
- The lighting in your room should not be too dark or too bright. Consider the angle of the light and how it may cast shadows on your face.
- The audience should be able to see you clearly, with most of your upper body being visible. Make sure the presenter does not overlap with the texts.

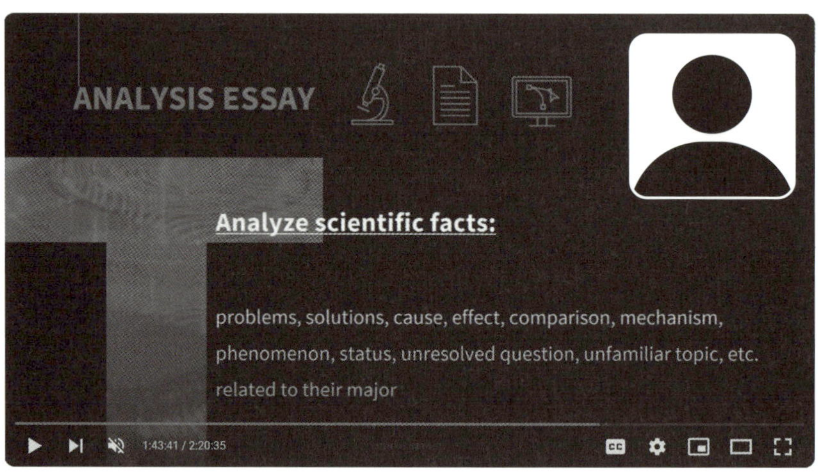

## B. Posture, Gestures and Eye Contact

- In order to appear confident to the audience, be sure to sit up straight and rest your hands gently on the desk when not gesturing. As with in-person presenting, do not slouch!
- Although gestures play less of a role in video presenting, they should still be included to make your speech look natural.
- As the audience will be mostly focused on your face, it is a good idea to consider a range of facial expressions to use in your speech. Like gestures, your facial expressions can help you to emphasize the contents of your speech.
- Over video, you cannot see the audience, but you should maintain consistent eye contact with the camera for most of the presentation.

## C. Voice

- Voice plays an important role when comparing video presenting to a live in-person presentation. Intonation, pace and the other elements covered in the voice section (see 4.1. Verbal Delivery skills). remain just as important.
- Signposting should be used more often in video presenting in order to draw the audience's attention to your visual aids. This will help maintain the audience's understanding of your presentation, in the way that gestures would help guide the audience in-person.

## 5. Visual Aids

Visual aids are tools and materials used to enhance and clarify the information presented during an academic talk. These aids can range from simple charts and graphs to multimedia, such as videos and animations. The use of visual aids in an academic presentation serves several purposes:

### Clarify and Emphasize Points

Visual aids can help clarify complex ideas or emphasize key points. They can illustrate concepts that might be difficult to explain with words alone.

### Engage the Audience

Visual aids can capture and maintain the audience's attention. An engaged audience is more likely to understand and retain the information presented.

### Organize Information

Visual aids can help organize information

in a structured and logical manner. This aids in the flow of the presentation and helps the audience follow along more easily.

## 5.1. Types of Visual Aids

The selection of an appropriate chart is crucial for the purpose of a presentation and the type of information being delivered. This chapter will introduce various types of charts and explain how to describe them in an academic presentation (Table 3.4).

**Table 3.4.** Common Types of Visual Aids

| Purpose | Types of charts |
|---|---|
| Comparison | Line charts and bar charts |
| Distribution | Histograms |
| Composition | Pie and area charts |
| Relationships | Scatter plots |

### A. Comparison

#### a. Bar Charts

A bar chart, also known as a bar graph, is used to compare quantities across different categories. The length or height of

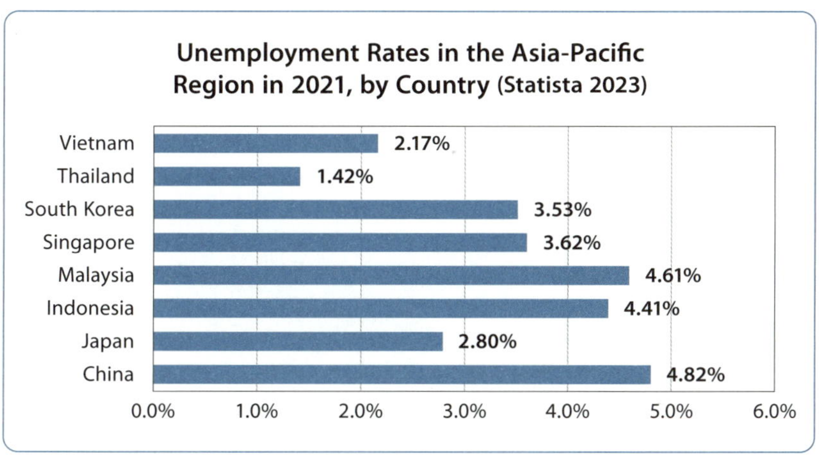


**Figure 3.5.** Bar Chart (Chart adapted from Statista, 2023)

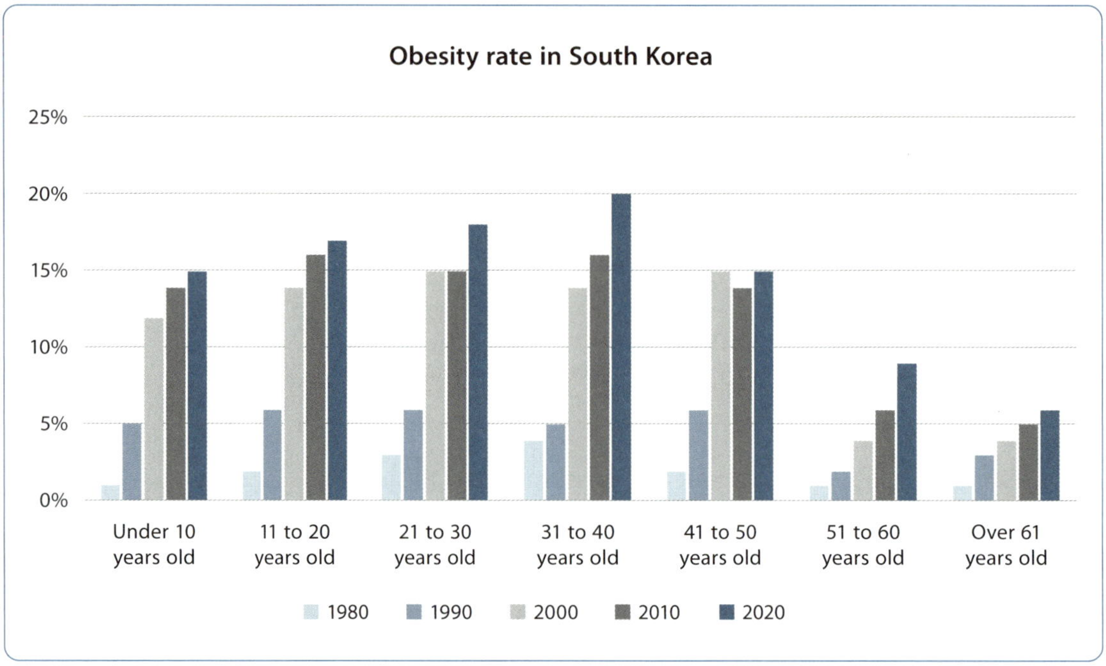


**Figure 3.6.** Obesity rate in South Korea between 1980 and 2020

each bar corresponds to its specific value or amount (Figures 3.5 & 3.6).

### b. Line Charts

A line chart is a type of graph that displays information as a series of data points connected by straight line segments. It is commonly used to visualize trends over intervals or time periods (Figure 3.7).

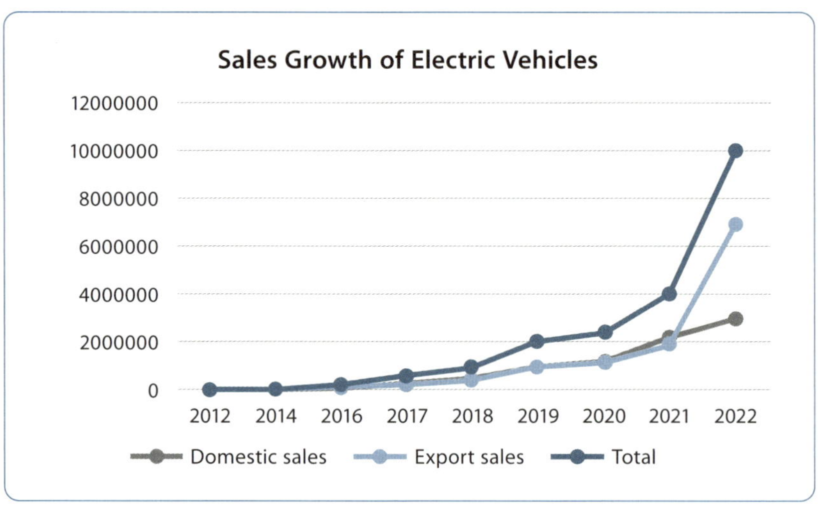


**Figure 3.7.** Sales Growth of Electric Vehicles

### B. Distribution: Histogram

A histogram shows the frequency distribution of values. Histograms are useful for noticing specific peaks and patterns in the information gathered (Figure 3.8).

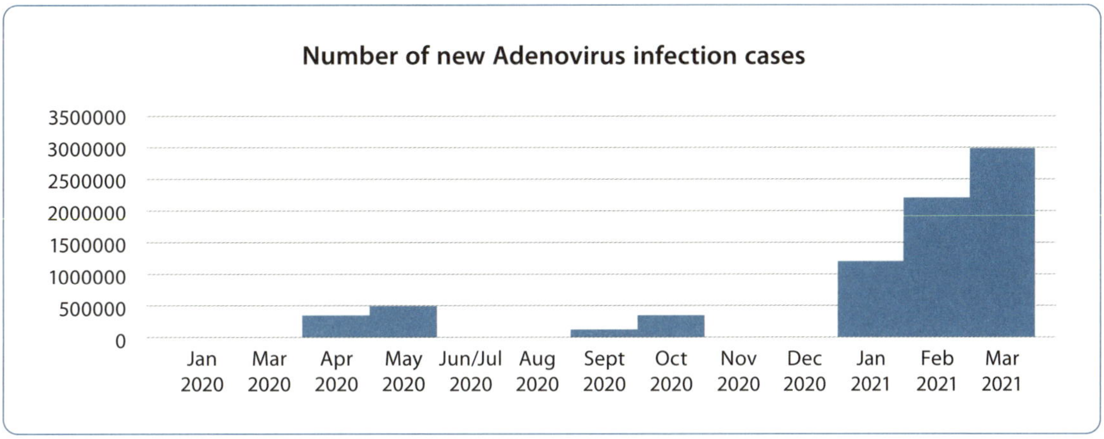


**Figure 3.8.** Number of new Adenovirus infection cases

### C. Composition

#### a. Pie charts

A pie chart is a circular graph that represents data by dividing a circle into proportional slices or sections. Each slice corresponds to a percentage or part of the whole data set (Figure 3.9).

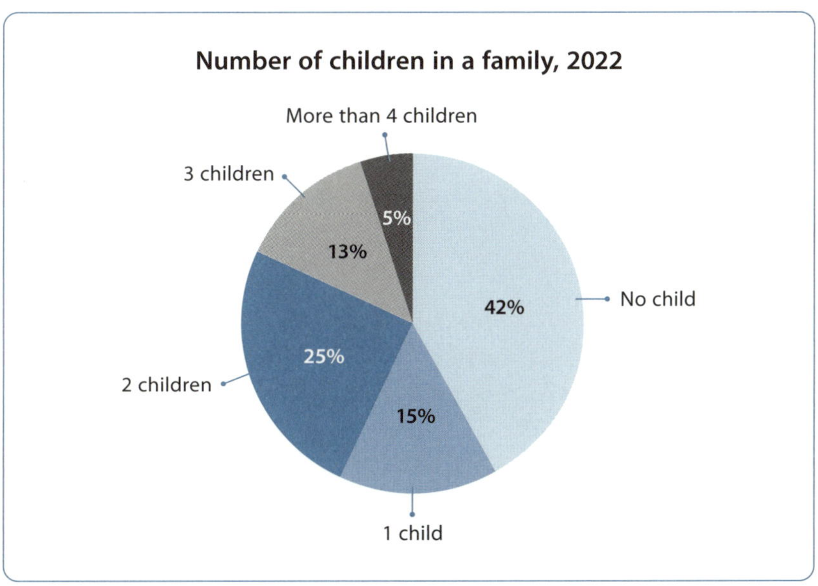


**Figure 3.9.** Number of children in a family, 2022

### b. Area Chart

An area chart is similar to a line chart, but fills the space to highlight the total quantity across segments. Colors or shades are used below the lines to show the distinct differences between the variables. In Figure 3.10, different color ranges of clothes are measured by their sales over one year.

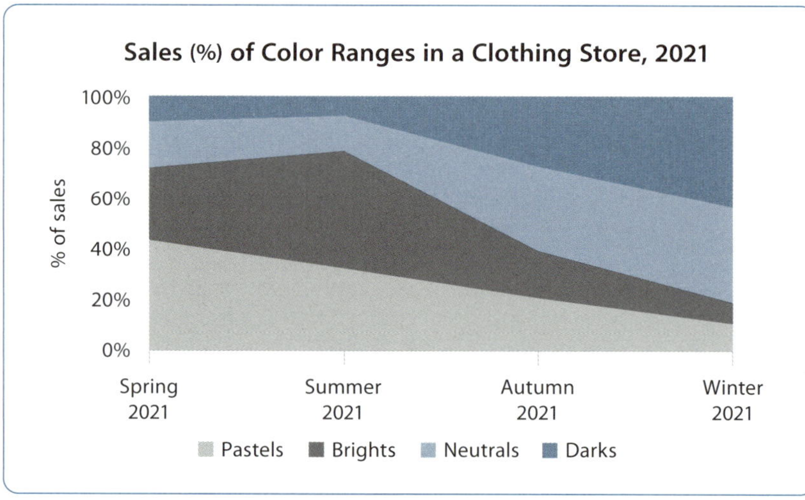


**Figure 3.10.** Sales (%) of Color ranges in a Clothing Store, 2021

## D. Showing Relationships: Scatter Plot

A scatter plot is a graph with dots that show how two sets of data relate to each other. Each dot represents a piece of data, with one set shown on the horizontal line and the other on the vertical line (Figure 3.11).

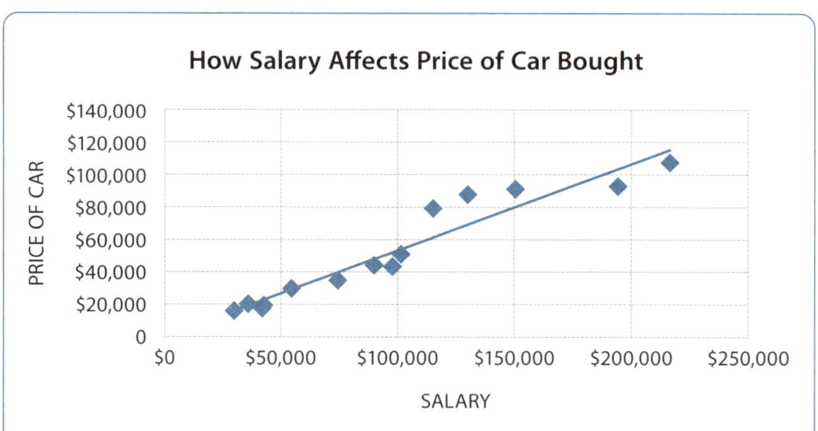


**Figure 3.11.** How salary affects price of car bought

## 5.2. How to Describe Visual Aids

When using a chart in your presentation to support your points, highlighting its key aspects is necessary. There are three steps to describing a chart.

**Step 1.** Begin by stating the title of the chart to provide context.

**Step 2.** Emphasize differences or similarities by comparing specific data points.

**Step 3.** Conclude with the overall significance or implication of the data for your main message.

***Example***

**Step 1.**

This line graph represents the 'Sales Growth of Electric Vehicles.'

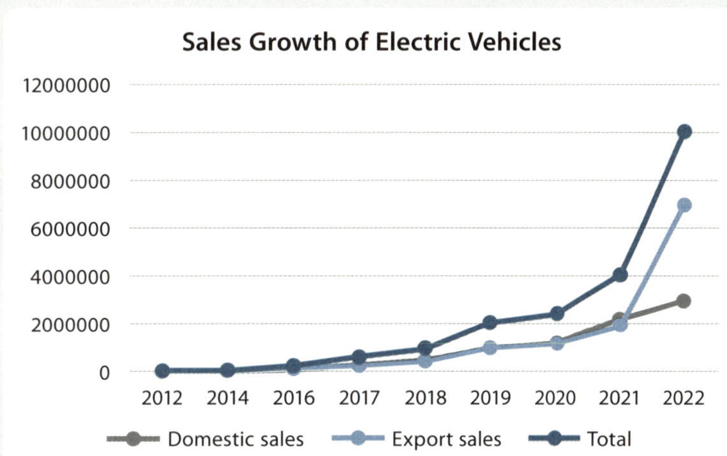


**Step 2.**

As you can see in this graph, the sales of both domestic and export sales have increased over the years, especially skyrocketed since 2020. Another interesting point is that export sales surpassed domestic sales after 2021.

**Step 3.**

This graph overall demonstrates that the sales of electric vehicles are likely to continue increasing.

## 5.3. Useful Language for Describing Charts and Graphs

When referring to data within charts, use various phrases to emphasize key points clearly.

### A. Language Used To Describe Changes

**Verbs:** rise, increase, grow, go up, improve, jump, surge, shoot up, soar, rocket
**Nouns:** a rise, an increase, growth, an upward/rising/increasing trend, an improvement, a jump, a surge

**Verbs:** fall, decrease, drop, decline, go down, slump, plummet
**Nouns:** a fall, a decrease, a decline, a downward trend, a slump

**No Change:** remain stable/constant, stay at the same level, stabilize
**Frequent Change:** fluctuate, fluctuation

**Top:** reach a peak, peak, reach its/their highest point
**Bottom:** reach/hit a low (point), hit/reach its/their lowest point, trough

*Example*

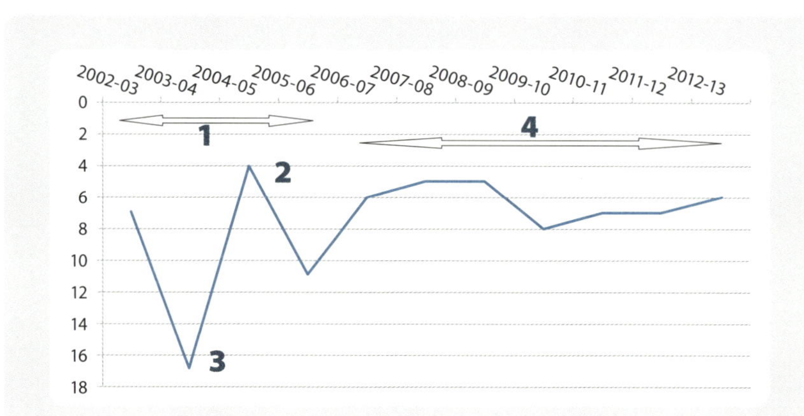

1) The final league position **fluctuates** between 2002 and 2006.
2) The final league position **peaked** in the 2004-2005 season.
3) The final league position reached its **lowest point** in the 2003-2004 season.
4) The final league position remained at **approximately the same level** between 2006 and 2013.

### B. Emphasizing Changes

**Adjectives:** *sharp, dramatic, sudden, rapid, significant, considerable, moderate, steady, gradual, slight, slow*
**Adverbs:** *sharply, dramatically, suddenly, rapidly, significantly, considerably, moderately, steadily, gradually, slightly, slowly*
**Prepositions:** *a rise* ***from*** *X* ***to*** *Y, an increase* ***of*** *X%* ***in*** *the variable, to fluctuate* ***between*** *X and Y, to decrease* ***by*** *X%*

### C. Expressing numbers

| Percentage | Fractions |
|---|---|
| 80% | four-fifths |
| 75% | three-quarters |
| 67% | two-thirds |
| 60% | three-fifths |
| 50% | half |
| 25% | a quarter |

| Percentage | Qualifier |
|---|---|
| 77% | **just over** three-quarters |
| 77% | **approximately** three quarters |
| 55% | **more than** half |
| 49% | **just under** half |
| 49% | **nearly** half |
| 32% | **almost** a third |

| 75% - 85% | 65% - 75% | 10% - 15% | 5% |
|---|---|---|---|
| a very large **majority** | a **significant proportion** | a **minority** | a very **small number** |

***Example***

"In this chart of Hanyang Students' fruit preferences, a **quarter of** students said they prefer bananas. Kiwi was the second most popular choice, selected by just **over a fifth** of the respondents. **A very small number** – only 3% - expressed a preference for figs."

**Hanyang Students' Fruit Preferences, 2023**
**(Source: Hanyang Cafeteria Services)**

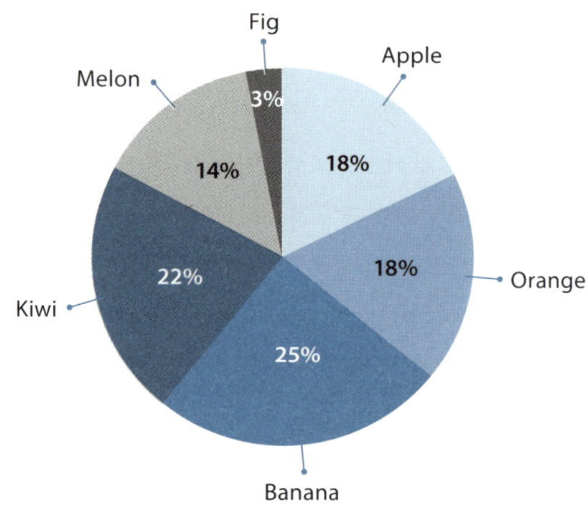


## 5.4. Transforming Written Content into Visual Data

Creating visual data from written contents allows for a more engaging and digestible presentation of information. Presenters can effectively convey complex ideas and ensure better audience comprehension by converting text into visual aids.

Look at the following hypothetical examples which include data. If you were to make charts to show these data points, what kind of chart would you use? How would you show the data in the most effective way?

**Example 1**

→ **Written content**

*A consumer rating website called Consumer Bites has been keeping track of trends in international drama series on popular streaming services. Here is what their data reveals:*

1. **The Crown:** The show had 5 million viewers for its premiere, then 4 million for the second week, and 3 million for weeks three and four.
2. **The Last of Us:** This series started strong with 5 million viewers in its first week, reached 6 million in the second week, and maintained 5 million viewers for weeks three and four.
3. **The Bridge:** While still popular, 'The Bridge' had slightly fewer viewers. It started with 2 million in its first week, dropped to 1 million for the second and third weeks, and had 500,000 viewers in the fourth week.
4. **Squid Game:** 'Squid Game' had a different trend. It began with 500,000 viewers for its premiere, then jumped to 1 million in the second week, 2 million in the third week, and finally reached 4 million viewers in its fourth week.

→ **Visual data**

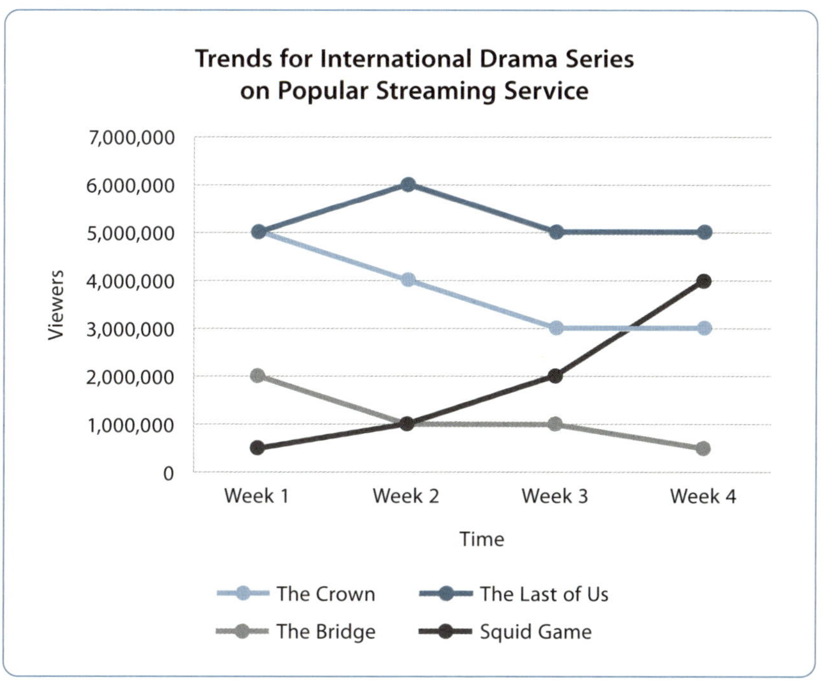


**Figure 3.12.** Trends for international drama series on popular streaming services

**Example 2**

→ **Written content**

*A popular website (PopBlog) ran a poll to find what peoples' worst fears were from a selection of five possibilities. Among the top five fears in the poll, 50 people stated that flying was their worst fear, 100 chose heights, 200 said spiders, 250 cited needles, and the worst fear was public speaking, with 400 people claiming it as their worst fear.*

→ **Visual data**

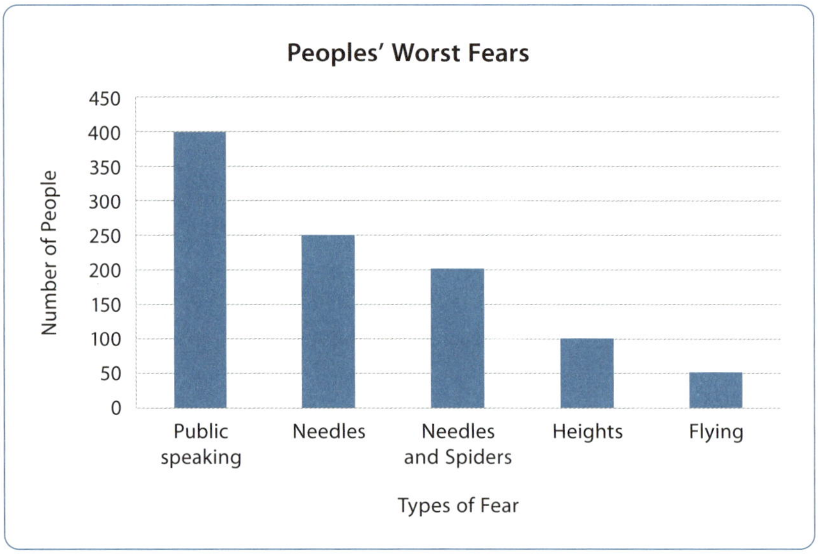


**Figure 3.13.** Types of Fear

## 5.5. Visual Design

When creating a visual aid, consider its appearance – this can include the choices of colors, the placement of items on the page, and the amount of information included. The following four strategies will help you enhance the quality of your visual materials.

**Contrast:** Highlighting differences in the elements of presentation slides can emphasize crucial information, and make the message clearer for the audience. The use of varied **colors**, **highlights**, **fonts**, and **text sizes** should be

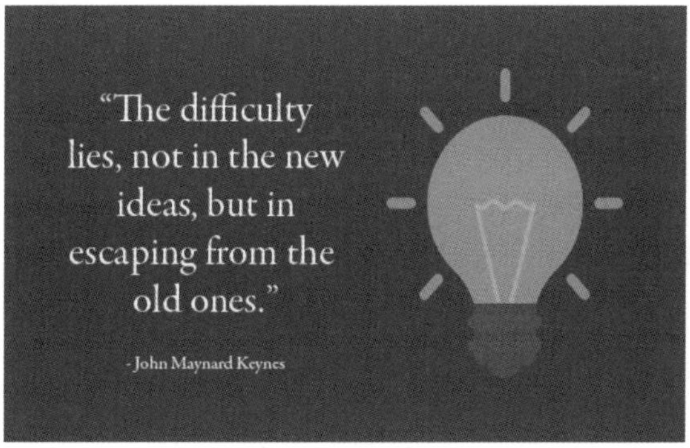


Figure 3.14. Contrast

thoughtfully designed (Figure 3.14).

**Repetition:** Repeating visual elements helps create unity and predictability across slides. Maintaining **consistency** in fundamental details, such as **font choice**, **background**, and **color scheme** can make the presentation look well-organized and appealing. Excessive variation between slides can be distracting.

**Layout:** Arrange the content of the presentation slides in a clear and logical manner. Avoid overcrowding the slide and consider the most intuitive way the audience might read the information, such as from left to right, top to bottom, or in a linear fashion. Compare the two slides below (Figure 3.15: A and B).

[A] [B]

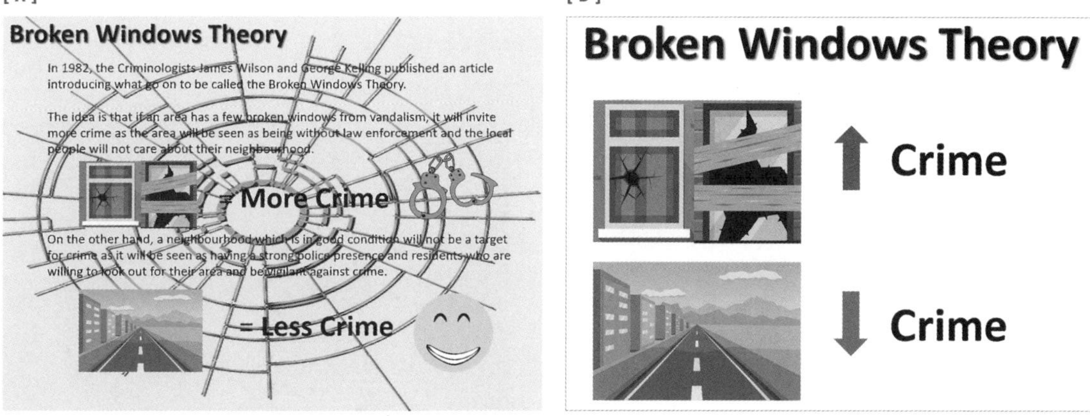


Figure 3.15. Broken Windows Theory: A. Overcrowded slide; B. Simplified slide

**Closeness:** Which items on a PPT slide are related? How can the relationship between different parts of the slides be demonstrated? Consider grouping items together to indicate order, significance, and cohesion. As can be seen in Figure 3.16, icons on the left are clustered together in a circle, representing demotivating factors. The 'profit loss' icon on the right is shown alone, to signify its importance as a consequence of those demotivating factors.

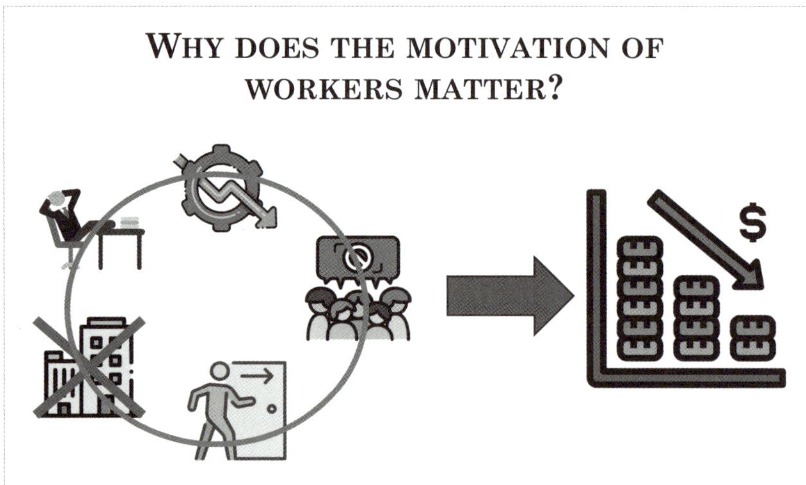


**Figure 3.16.** Why does the Motivation of Workers Matter?

## 5.6. Referencing Figures and Images in Presentations

### A. Citation in Visual Aids

For each image used on visual aids, you need to add a **citation** below the image on the slide unless it is a free stock image. Make sure to add the figure number, title, author, and year (See Figure 3.17).

**Figure 3.17.** Irises (Van Gogh, V, 1889)

### B. Reference List

All citations should be presented in a comprehensive list on the final slide of the visual aids (Figure 3.18). The format for these citations should align with writing conventions, such as those outlined in APA, 7th edition.

## References


Gagné, M., Forest, J., Vansteenkiste, M., Crevier-Braud, L., Van den Broeck, A., Aspeli, A. K., ... Westbye, C. (2015). The multidimensional work motivation scale: validation evidence in seven languages and nine countries. *European Journal of Work and Organizational Psychology, 24*(2), 178–196. https://doi.org/10.1080/1359432X.2013.877892

Glassdoor (2021) "11 Tips for Motivating Millennials." Glassdoor. https://www.glassdoor.com/employers/blog/11-tips-for-motivating-millennials/

Hall, M (2020) "How to Navigate Job Hunting during a Period of Layoffs and Extreme Unemployment". Forbes. https://www.forbes.com/sites/markhall/2020/04/05/job-hunting-during-unemployment/?sh=7bcf6ea724d3

Haryono, S., Supardi, S & Udin, U. (2020). The effect of training and job promotion on work motivation and its implications on job performance: Evidence from Indonesia. *Management Science Letters*, 10(9), 2107-2112.

Mahmoud, A., Fuxman, L., Mohr, I., Reisel, W., and Grigoriou, N. (2021). "We aren't your reincarnation!" workplace motivation across X, Y and Z generations. *International Journal of Manpower. 42.* 193-209. 10.1108/IJM-09-2019-0448.

Morris, V (2021) "Gen X at Work: How to Keep them Happy and Productive". Workzinga. https://workzinga.com/job-motivation-for-gen-x-employees/

Patel, D (2017) "8 Ways Generation Z will Differ from Millennials in the Workplace". Forbes. https://www.forbes.com/sites/deeppatel/2017/09/21/8-ways-generation-z-will-differ-from-millennials-in-the-workplace/?sh=767921ad76e5

Images from www.flaticon.com


**Figure 3.18.** Reference list slide

# 1. Annotation

| Title of the text | |
|---|---|
| Author(s) | |
| Publication information* | |
| Key points | 1.<br>2.<br>3. |
| Evaluation** | |
| Relevance to your essay** | |

* **Publication information**: date, journal/book title, and page numbers

** **Evaluation**: Consider the following questions.
- Are the arguments well-supported?
- Is the evidence convincing?
- Is it logically written?

*** **Relevance to your essay**: Explain how this text is relevant to your own essay or research. Discuss how you might use the information or ideas from this text in your academic work.

## 2. Model Essay

### Success of Australia's Tourism

Many successful industries contribute to the GDP of Australia. One such industry, the tourism industry, contributes 3.2 per cent to Australia's income and is responsible for employing 4.9 per cent of the population (Department of Resources, Energy and Tourism, 2020). Australia, a land of contrasts and wonders, has consistently been a magnet for travelers worldwide. From the iconic Sydney Opera House and the Great Barrier Reef to the mysteries of the Outback, the country offers a range of attractions that few places can match. While its popularity among tourists is undeniable, pinpointing the exact reasons for this appeal requires a closer look. The success of Australia's tourism can be attributed to breathtaking landscapes and unique wildlife.

Australia's unique geological and ecological features make it a particularly attractive tourist location. First, Australia's Tourism Commissioner states that 67% of tourists from 2010 to 2014 cited extraordinary natural phenomena as a significant motivating reason for their visit (Figure 1) (DRET, 2020). For example, the Uluru-Kata Tjuta National Park is listed as one of the few World Heritage properties recognized for both its natural and cultural values (Georgiou, 2017, p. 21). Uluru is acknowledged as the world's largest monolith (DRET, 2020), and the formation is so rare that it captivates the world with its sheer size, vibrant colors, and cultural significance. Another reason that Australia is attractive to overseas tourists is that it has over 10,000 miles of white sandy beaches, some of the world's best surfing conditions and a climate that allows comfortable swimming throughout the year (DRET, 2020). Unique geological features and ecology create landforms which are key components of Australia's appeal to tourists.

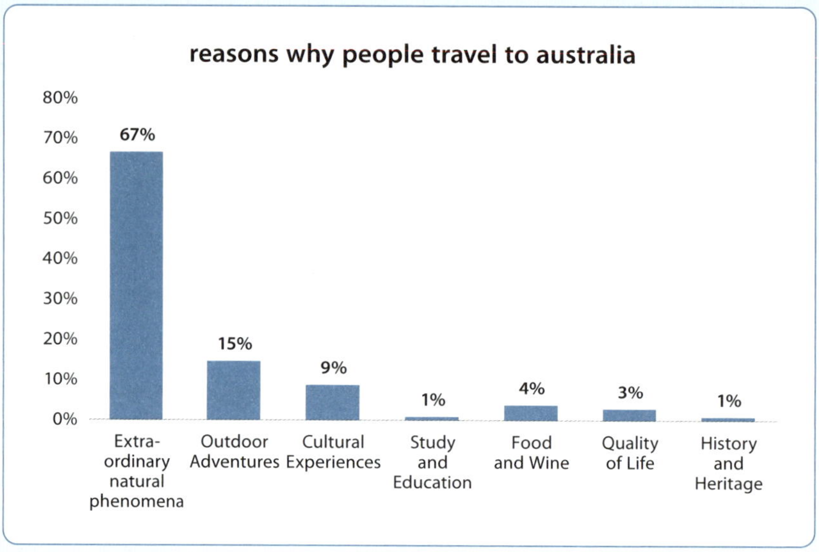


**Figure 1.** Reasons why people travel to Australia

Australia is also renowned for its unique and diverse wildlife, making it a fascinating destination for wildlife lovers. One of the most iconic natural wonders is the Great Barrier Reef, which spans over 2,300 kilometers. As seen in Figure 1, it ranks as the most popular tourist destination in Australia. This remarkable coral ecosystem offers colorful underwater scenery that attracts snorkelers and divers, providing opportunities to encounter a diverse array of aquatic species, from dazzling clownfish to majestic sea turtles. Beyond the aquatic realm, Australia is also home to some of the world's most distinctive land creatures (DRET, 2020). Exploring the remarkable wildlife of Australia provides a unique opportunity for travelers to connect with nature. For instance, kangaroos and koalas symbolize Australia's animals and observing these animals in their natural habitat gives tourists an unforgettable experience. Such natural wonders and diverse wildlife make Australia an extraordinary destination for those who seek to experience the beauty of the natural world.

Some may argue that the significant physical separation from the world's population hubs can be an inhibiting factor for the success of the tourist industry. It is true that Australia is one of the most remote countries on Earth, and overseas travelers spend an average of 17 hours reaching Australia, a duration twice as long as the travel time to other geographically distinct destinations (Proctor & Thomas, 2014). However, it may not negatively impact tourist numbers as much as initially considered due to the opportunity for visitors to explore various unique geographic features in one trip within a safe cultural context. While Australia may receive fewer total visitors, each tourist tends to spend three times more time compared to the average duration spent in a single country, excluding the USA (DRET, 2020). The country compensates the physical obstacle by encouraging visitors to allocate more of their vacation budget for a distinctive experience. Consequently, Australia remains a premier destination that offers unparalleled and unforgettable adventures despite its geographical challenges.

In conclusion, Australia's immense appeal to tourists arises from its unparalleled geological features and diverse wildlife. While the nation benefits substantially from the tourism sector, the challenges of the geographic distance from major global hubs were not discussed in this essay. Also, the research was limited to the years 2010 to 2014, and a broader timeframe may offer varied insights. Future research could examine evolving tourist preferences, especially in the post-pandemic era, and assess the potential impact of virtual tourism. Ultimately, despite its remoteness, Australia's ability to provide a unique, consolidated experience ensures tourists find the journey worth their time and resources. (812 words)

## References


Brown, J. M., & Parker, R. E. (2017). Australia's distinctive land creatures: A comprehensive guide. *Journal of Wildlife Research, 42*(3), 211-226. https://doi.org/10.105/j.wr.2017.32.03

Department of Resources, Energy and Tourism (DRET) (2020). *Australia tourism and overseas statistics and status*. https://arena.gov.au/funding/department-of-resources-energy-and-tourism/

Georgiou, A. A. (2007). The most attractive tourist areas in Australia. *Journal of Australian Tourism, 4*(5), 43-49. https://doi.org/10.345964kl30298as

Proctor, P., & Thomas, A. (2004). *Australia's tourism and the world's perspective*. Brisbane Publishing company.

Smith, A. (2020). *Wildlife wonders of Australia. National Geographic Society*. Retrieved Apr 3, 2023, from https://www.nationalgeographic.com/travel/article/stunning-natural-wonders

UNESCO. (2019). *Great Barrier Reef World Heritage Area*. UNESCO World Heritage Centre. Retrieved Mar 30, 2023, from https://whc.unesco.org/en/list/154/

# 3. Example Essays from Students (HASS)

## Revolutionizing Fashion Marketing: The Power of AI Technology

Artificial Intelligence (AI) technology has significantly impacted the marketing industry, particularly in fashion marketing. AI refers to the development of computer systems that can perform tasks that typically require human intelligence, such as speech recognition, decision-making, and natural language processing. With its ability to analyze vast amounts of data quickly and accurately, AI has become an indispensable tool for fashion brands looking to gain insights into customer behavior and enhance the shopping experience. According to a recent report, fashion companies are expecting to deploy AI to redefine interactions and engagement with customers (Anderson et al., 2017). This paper will explore three innovations created by AI technology in fashion marketing: providing personalized experiences, AI chatbots, and virtual try-on technology.

To begin with, AI technology has made fashion marketing evolve in a more personalized way. Personalized marketing is a method that provides services optimized for each consumer's characteristics. It is a way to understand customers' tastes and interests and deliver messages that they might be interested in. By using AI, they can quickly determine what content to target customers and which channel to employ at what moment, thanks to the data collected and generated by its algorithms. (Haleem et al, 2022). These AI algorithms create personalized recommendations based on each consumer's preferences by analyzing digital information from various sources such as social media, online shopping websites, and mobile applications. AI technology has enabled such experiences at scale, leading to increased customer satisfaction and retention.

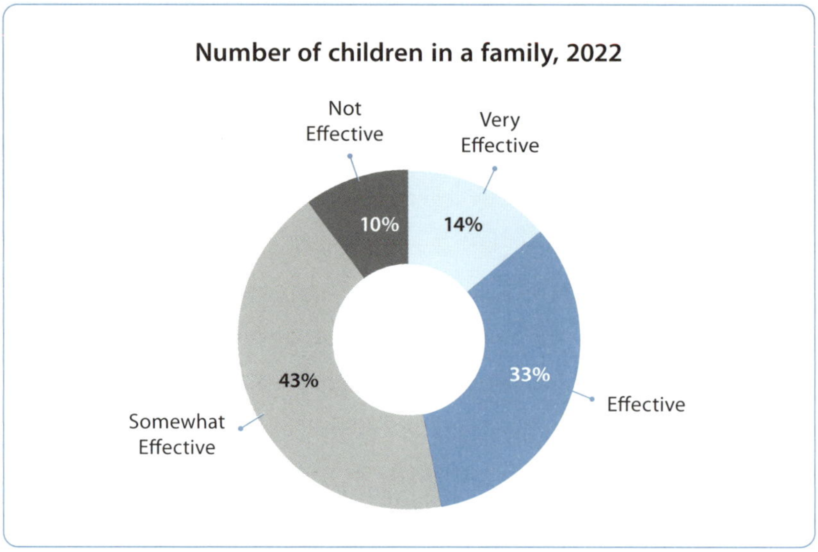


**Figure 1.** Results of customer satisfaction survey with chatbots (Sachs, 2019)

In addition, AI-powered chatbots help fashion brands build better interaction with their customers. Chatbots can be defined as AI-based computer programs that can talk to people and be inactive in communication (Bariş, 2020). They can communicate with customers in real-time, answer their questions, and provide personalized recommendations. The chatbots are available round the clock, so customers can seek assistance anytime. This means they can save customer's time and effort. Figure 1 demonstrates that chatbots ensure quick responses and at least some degree of customer satisfaction, with almost half of the survey respondents claiming chatbot interactions to be either very effective or effective (Sachs, 2019). Additionally, chatbots also can collect and analyze customer data, such as inquiries and preferences, to gain insights into customer behavior and trends. This helps fashion brands make data-driven decisions and tailor their offerings.

Further, AI-powered virtual try-on technology is revolutionizing the way of fashion marketing, especially in the offline retail business. The technology allows customers to see how a garment looks on them without physically trying it on. Popular fashion brands including L'Oréal, Baume, Sephora, Adidas, Nike and Snap are opting for try-on technology in order to improve the connectivity with customers and gain a competitive advantage in the market (Ghodhbani et al., 2022). It is reported that virtual try-on affects the sales results: the average sales per customer increased by 14,000 won (13USD) (Hwangbo et al., 2020). Moreover, it is more likely to reduce the number of returns, which is beneficial for both customers and fashion brands.

In conclusion, AI technology enables fashion brands to offer personalized marketing, interactive communication, and virtual try-on experience that increases customer engagement and satisfaction. However, this paper only covered the positive role of Artificial Intelligence in marketing and there are risks of data bias and privacy concerns for the use of personal data. It is crucial to look into the issues closely to maintain customer trust. Through further examination, the positive influence of AI technology on fashion marketing can be further enhanced, leading to more personalized, engaging, and successful interactions between fashion brands and customers.

## References

Andersson, J., Kappelmark. S., Berg, A., Drageset, M., Hedrich, S., & Amed, I. (2017). *The state of fashion 2018*. McKinsey & Company. https://www.mckinsey.com/~/media/mckinsey/industries/retail/our insights/renewed optimism for the fashion industry/the-state-of-fashion-2018-final.pdf

Barış, A. (2020). A new business marketing tool: Chatbot. *GSI Journals Serie B: Advancements in Business and Economics, 3*(1), 31-46.

Ghodhbani, H., Neji, M., Razzak, I., & Alimi, A. (2022). You can try without visiting: A comprehensive survey on virtually try-on outfits. *Multimedia Tools Application, 81*, 19967–19998

Haleem, A., Javaid, M., Qadri, M. A., Singh, R. P., & Suman, R. (2022). Artificial intelligence (AI) applications for marketing: A literature-based study. *International Journal of Intelligent Networks, 3*, 119–132.

Hwangbo, H., Kim, E. H., Lee, S., & Jang, Y. J. (2020). Effects of 3D virtual "Try-On" on online sales and customers' purchasing experiences. *IEEE Access, 8*, 189479-189489.

Sachs, S. (2019). 4 chatbot success metrics to bolster CX. *Tech Target*. https://www.techtarget.com/searchcustomer experience/answer/4-chatbot-success-metrics-to-bolster-CX

## Konglish Should be Accepted as a Dialect of English

"I'm fine thank you, and you? [aɪm paɪn dæŋkyu ændə ju?]." This is a typical example of how English teachers in Korea teach their students to respond to the simple question: "How are you?" This is called *Konglish*, Korean-style English, and that it can sound unnatural to native English speakers. As *Hallyu*, or the Korean wave, has spread across the world, native speakers have become aware of Konglish and it has often been attacked and mocked, even by Koreans themselves, for its unique pronunciation and vocabulary. However, Konglish should be accepted as a dialect of English with regard to language transfer and creativity of language.

Konglish should be recognized as a dialect of English based on language transfer, a phenomenon through which properties of a first language (L1) are carried over into a second language (L2). Konglish is known for its unique pronunciation due to the differences between Korean and English linguistics. In particular, the phonological system of Korean is distinct from that of English (Lee 1981). For example, the phonemes /f/, /ʒ/, and /θ/ do not exist in the Korean phonological system. As an alternative, Koreans tend to replace them with their native phonemes such as /p/, /dʒ/, and /d/, as they produce similar sounds. Konglish is not the only language that has a unique accent; every dialect has its own accent due to language transfer. For example, Grolman (2021) observes that Indians tend to pronounce 'vet' as [wet], and 'zero' as [ʤi:ro] because there is no /v/ and /z/ in languages in India. Furthermore, Irish English pronunciation of /θ/ sounds closer to /t/, and Scottish English pronounces the /w/ in 'which' as /hw/. These phonological differences are a key area of English language study (Cao & Jun, 2017), and thus proving their acceptance as dialects. In short, language transfer from Korean to English has created examples of nonstandard pronunciation of English vocabulary, thus creating a specialised version of English named Konglish.

The creativity of language is another foundation for acknowledging Konglish as a dialect of English. Language itself is flexible and constantly changing, and the formation of different dialects of English proves the creativity of the cultures using that language. That is, every dialect possesses its own set of vocabulary that is not commonly employed in other regions. For instance, Australian English features numerous distinctive expressions, prompting the creation of the Australian Oxford Dictionary to elucidate these terms (Oxford University Press, 2004). Similarly, Konglish has its unique vocabulary, such as *'fighting,' 'handphone,' 'dica,'* and *'skinship,'* and these serve as a reflection of cultural identity and linguistic diversity. Moreover, Yoon (2022) notes that certain Konglish terms such as 'fighting' and 'skinship' have already earned a place in the Oxford English Dictionary (OED, 2022), and there exists the potential for Konglish words to attain standard status over time. Kachru's concept of World Englishes supports this perspective, emphasizing the importance of familiarizing students with various types of English rather than adhering solely to a relative standard (cited in Kilickaya, 2009). In the context of global communication in the 'Expanding Circle' of English learners, accepting dialectical variants becomes imperative.

Despite the aforementioned justifications, there are detractors to the idea of Konglish being accepted as an English dialect. Park Moo-jong, a Korea Times columnist, argues that Konglish is a form of broken English because words such as *'fighting,' 'handphone,'* and *'dica'* are used exist exclusively in South Korea (Park, 2015). However, his argument fails to take into consideration the ever-changing and diverse characteristics of language. The various ways in which a language can alter reveal the cultural identity of different regions. As mentioned above, some of the vocabulary Park gave as examples of broken English have already been added to the Oxford English Dictionary. Therefore, Park's critique is short-sighted and dismissive. Given the parallels between English dialects and Konglish, it becomes evident that labeling Konglish as merely a form of 'broken' English is unjust and Jeon

(1996) contends that there is no such thing as incorrect language.

In conclusion, Konglish is a dialectical form of English spoken by native Korean speakers and has faced attack because of its nonstandard accent and vocabulary. However, Konglish shares similarities with other dialects of English with respect to language transfer and the diverse, flexible and creative characteristics of language.  For these reasons, Konglish should not be disregarded; rather, it should be accepted as a dialect of English. Konglish deserves recognition as a legitimate form of English.

## References


Cao, R., & Jun, S. (2017). Phonological differences between received pronunciation and standard Scottish English. *In Advances in Social Science, Education and Humanities Research (Vol. 113).*

Grolman, M. B. (2021). Phonetic peculiarities of the English language in India. *International Journal of Society, Culture & Language, 9*(1), 102-110.

Jeon, E. C. (1996). *Study on American English dialects* [Master's dissertation, Graduate School of Kyeonggi University]. RISS. https://www.riss.kr/search/detail/DetailView.do?p_mat_type=be54d9b8bc7cdb09&control_no=d89178454be113b5

Kilickaya, F. (2009). World Englishes, English as an international language and applied linguistics. *English Language Teaching, 2*(3), 35-38.

Oxford University Press. (2004). *Australian Oxford dictionary* ($2^{nd}$ ed.). Oxford University Press.

Park, M. J. (2015, February 26). Stubborn mistakes in use of English terms. *The Korea Times*. http://www.koreatimes.co.kr/www/opinion/2019/12/636_174220.html

Yoon, H. S. (2022). Analysis of Korean vocabulary listed in Oxford English Dictionary (OED): From the perspective of Korean education. *The Society of Korean Culture and Convergence, 44*(2), 127-146. https://doi.org/10.33645/cnc.2022.02.44.2.127

## 4. Example Essays from Students (STEM)

### Pros and Cons of Drone Delivery

Delivery services are usually carried by truck or motorcycle and companies in many countries are now switching to drone delivery, rather than ground delivery. In 2019, an American company Wing became the first in the world to commercialize drone delivery [1]. Drone delivery boasts a range of advantages but it also has disadvantages, accidents causing damage, for example. This essay will discuss three advantages of drone delivery in terms of costs, delivery time, and environmental impact, as well as three disadvantages: influence of weather, security risk, and restrictions in range.

Drone delivery can present companies and customers with several advantages. First of all, drone delivery is lower in cost than truck delivery. Drones can reduce delivery costs because of cheaper drone technology and their ability to travel longer distances in less time, saving fuel and reducing the cost per mile [2~6]. The trucks usually used for delivery are light duty trucks, which cost between $25,000 and $45,000. On the other hand, a research group spent less than $100 building their own drones, and they showed that a drone powered by a 2200 milliampere-hour battery set to fly for 25 minutes could fly over 15km [6]. The second advantage of drone delivery is that it is faster than ground delivery [2~5]. Currently, if customers use a delivery service within South Korea, it may take a few days to arrive, while next day delivery is possible with only a few companies and products. However, in other countries, there have been some cases where goods have been delivered in a shorter time through a drone delivery service. For example, Amazon Prime Air set a goal of completing deliveries within 30 minutes [1] and even there was a case where delivery was completed in 15 minutes [8]. Finally, drone delivery is eco-friendly. Drones do not emit carbon because they operate on batteries, and fewer carbon emissions make the natural environment safe from harmful greenhouse gases [2~3]. As

Figure 1 shows, transportation accounted for the largest share of the five sectors of the United States economy in 2021 [9]. This means that carbon emissions can be reduced if delivery services are replaced by drones. These are just a few examples of the various benefits provided by drone delivery.

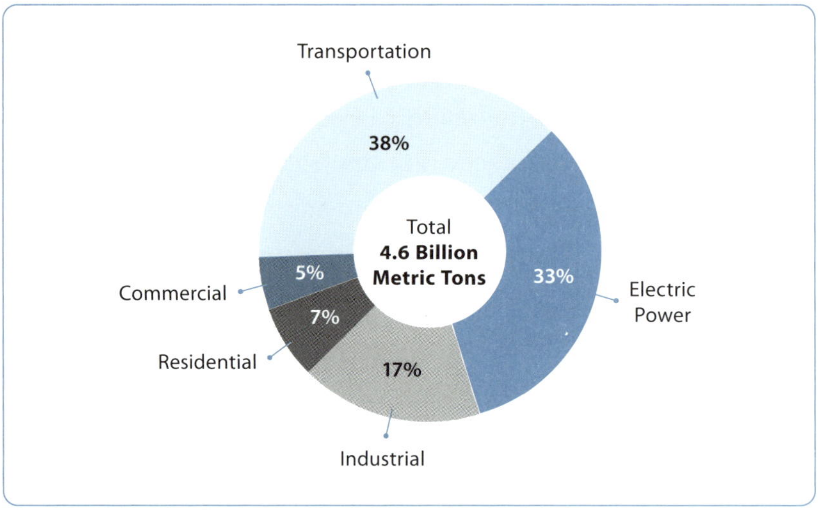


**Figure 1.** Energy-Related Emissions of Carbon Dioxide by Economic Sector in United States, 2021 [8]

Drone delivery is not without its limitations and there are three distinct disadvantages. First of all, drone delivery is subject to weather conditions. Drones can drift in multiple directions by the wind. Also, wind affects the rate of battery consumption and the operational range of a drone. It is reported that if the wind speed exceeds 12 mph, a drone will not be able to fly [5, 10]. For instance, in the United States, a Facebook drone crashed in Arizona due to strong winds [11]. Furthermore, rain can deteriorate product quality and cause drones to malfunction [5]. Another disadvantage is that drone delivery is risky in terms of security. Drone networks share more information than existing wireless networks, which means drones can be hacked and personal information may leak. Leaked personal information can then be sold to criminals, causing further harm to consumers [4, 12]. Furthermore, people's privacy can be invaded at any time, by having recordings and pictures taken without their permission.

According to the Canadian Public Safety, unmanned aerial vehicle (UAV) technology has been connected to blackmail and fraudulent acts of threatening to release personal photos or videos taken in the air without the victim's knowledge [12]. Finally, the range for drone delivery is restricted. The inescapably lightweight batteries on aerial drones cannot supply enough power for long distance or heavy payloads. Current drones can only carry up to 11lbs of weight [13] and carrying loads heavier than 11lbs may shorten the drone's original operating range or render the drone unable to fly. Overall, it is clear that the use of drones for delivery services has advantages, but companies and customers must pay attention to the disadvantages too.

In conclusion, the conveniences of drone delivery include lower cost, rapid delivery, and minimized carbon release, while the drawbacks are related to the weather, security risks, and the drone's restricted range. Drone delivery has been commercialized only recently, just few countries have commercialized drone delivery and most of the research about drone delivery comes from the United States. Therefore, there is a need for more comprehensive international research to provide a broader understanding of the drone delivery systems. If the development of drone delivery technology continues, cross-border distance deliveries will be able to be carried out in a fraction of the time, creating a better service for companies and their customers.

## References


[1] J. Elias, "Alphatbet's Wing launches first commercial drone delivery", *CNBC*, October 18, 2019 [Online], Available: https://www.cnbc.com/2019/10/18/alphabets-wing-launches-first-commercial-drone-delivery.html. [Accessed: May 14, 2023]

[2] B. Alkouz, B. Shahzaad, and A. Bouguettaya, "Service-based drone delivery," *2021 IEEE 7th International Conference on Collaboration and Internet Computing (CIC)*, 2021. [Online], Available: https://arxiv.org/pdf/2201.00277.pdf. [Accessed: March 18, 2023]

[3] A. Ankh-El, "Automatic Drone Delivery System." *Diss. Alabama Agricultural and Mechanical University*, 2021, [Online], Available: https://www.proquest.com/docview/2605609359?pq-origsite=gscholar&fromopenview=true. [Accessed: March 19, 2023]

[4] W. Xie, C. Chen, and J. Sithipolvanichgul, "Understanding e-commerce customer behaviors to use drone delivery services: A privacy calculus view," *Cogent Business & Management*, vol. 9, no. 1, 2022. [Online], Available: https://www.tandfonline.com/doi/pdf/10.1080/23311975.2022.2102791. [Accessed: April 2, 2023]

[5] X. Liu, M. Ahmed, M. Khan, and M. Khan, "Get the door. it's drone: The Future of Flying Food Deliveries", 2018. [Online], Available: https://www.chrie.org/assets/docs/JHTC-case-notes/JHTC-vol-7/JHTC_Vol7Issue1_Khan_case.pdf. [Accessed: April 3, 2023]

[6] L. P. Koh, and S. A. Wich. "Dawn of drone ecology: low-cost autonomous aerial vehicles for conservation." *Tropical Conservation Science*, vol. 5, no. 2, pp. 121-132. [Online], Available: https://journals.sagepub.com/doi/pdf/10.1177/194008291200500202. [Accessed: April 6, 2023]

[7] "How Much Does a New Box Truck Cost?", *CostOwl.com*, March 29, 2022. [Online], Available: https://www.costowl.com/automotive/commercial-construction/auto-box-truck-new-cost/. [Accessed: April 30, 2023]

[8] R. Min. "Amazon and Alphabet unit Wing Begin drone

deliveries in parts of the US." *Euronews.next*. [Online], Available: https://www.euronews.com/next/2022/10/06/amazon-and-alphabet-unit-wing-begin-drone-deliveries-in-parts-of-the-us. [Accessed: April 16, 2023]

[9] L. Swagel, "Emissions of Carbon Dioxide in the Transportation Sector", *Congressional Budget Office*, December, 2022. [Online], Available: https://www.cbo.gov/publication/58861. [Accessed: April 25, 2023]

[10] B. Shahzaad, A. Bouguettaya, S. Mistry, and A. G. Neiat, "Resilient composition of drone services for delivery," *Future Generation Computer Systems*, vol. 115, pp. 335–350, 2021. [Online], Available: https://arxiv.org/pdf/2009.09549.pdf. [Accessed: April 2, 2023]

[11] "Report: Facebook drone crash in Arizona caused by strong wind gust", *KTAR.com*, December 19, 2016. [Online], Available: https://ktar.com/story/1371894/facebook-drone-crash-arizona-wind-gust/. [Accessed: May 6, 2023]

[12] J. P. Yaacoub, H. Noura, O. Salman, and A. Chehab, "Security analysis of drones systems: Attacks, Limitations, and recommendations," *Internet of Things*, vol. 11, p. 100218, 2020. [Online], Available: https://www.ncbi.nlm.nih.gov/pmc/articles/PMC7206421/. [Accessed: April 25, 2023]

[13] I. Singh, "New A2Z pelican delivery drone can fly 25 miles with 11 lbs," *DroneDJ*, [Online], Available: https://dronedj.com/2023/05/02/a2z-delivery-drone-pelican/. [Accessed: May 7, 2023]

* IEEE referencing style is used in this example essay.

## Advantages of Small Modular Reactors

Global environmental movement efforts have been continued to achieve net-zero carbon emissions. Among them, interest in nuclear energy has increased as it is a low-carbon energy source capable of generating large-scale electricity. A small modular reactor (SMR) is considered as a complementary solution to large nuclear power plants due to its smaller and the potential to integrate its electrical output in a single facility. For this reason, it is attracting significant attention from both the government and major companies such as DOOSAN and Samsung C&T (Cho, 2022). As shown in Figure 1, the SMR market size is expected to grow worldwide. In the context of the ongoing development, this paper will compare large nuclear power plants and SMRs, focusing on the advantages of SMR in terms of safety, flexibility, and cost.

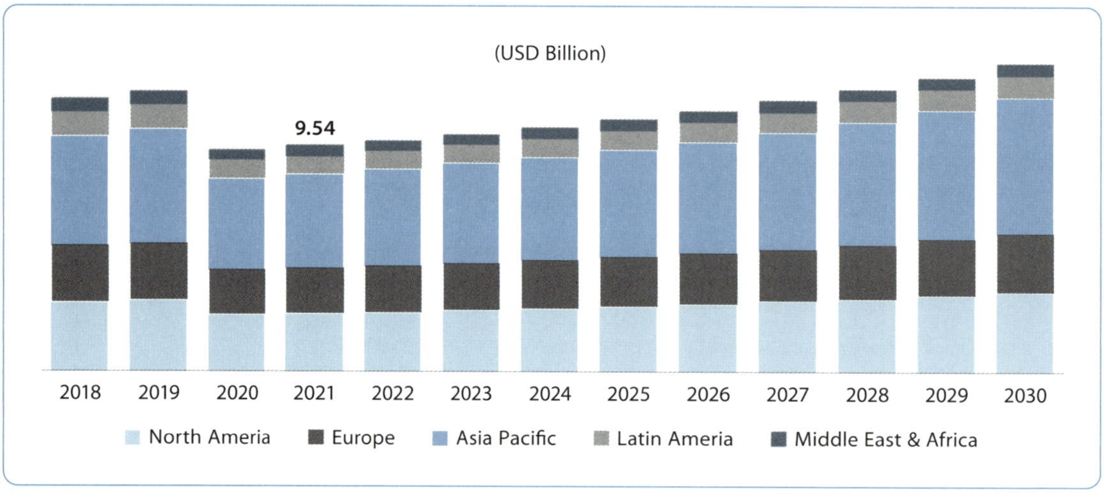


**Figure 1.** Small Modular Reactor market size by region (Polaris Market research, 2022)

First, SMR is safer than a large nuclear power plant. In a large nuclear power plant, main equipment is connected by pipe, but SMR is integrated into one without pipe connections (Korea Hydro & Nuclear Power, 2021). Since pipe cracks do not occur in SMR, the risk of pipe break accidents, which are representative reactor accidents, can be eliminated. In addition, SMR is designed with a passive safety concept (Liou, 2021), so it can minimize human intervention by removing residual heat through natural convection in the event of an accident. On the other hand, large nuclear power plants are designed with an active safety concept (Liou, 2021), so they are more likely to be at high risk of accidents as humans can fail to operate. As a result of its integrated and passive design, SMR can be 1000 times safer than a large nuclear power plant (Korea Hydro & Nuclear Power, 2021).

Second, SMR is more geographically flexible than a large nuclear power plant. Large nuclear power plants are built near the coast, because they require a large amount of cooling water to cool heated reactors. By contrast, SMR can be constructed anywhere, including inland (Liou, 2021), because it uses a passive cooling method through natural convection. Due to the geographical flexibility of SMR, it can be used in various places other than electricity generation. For example, SMR can be used to power desalination plants, which convert sea water into fresh water. Furthermore, it is also used in military devices such as bases and submarines, which could improve security by reducing dependence on external power sources. Thus, SMR is very valuable in fields where large nuclear power plants cannot be applied.

Finally, SMR requires lower capital cost than a large nuclear power plant. In large nuclear power plants, manufacturing begins on site using pipe connections (Korea Hydro & Nuclear Power, 2021). On the other hand, SMR is designed as a modular type, so it is manufactured completely in a factory and then transported to a site, installed (Liou, 2021). Therefore, construction of large nuclear power plants is more complex and takes longer than SMR, so construction costs are higher. Approximately, the construction cost of one SMR is estimated to be about 1 trillion won while the construction cost of a large nuclear power plant is estimated to be 3 trillion won to 4 trillion won (Ministry of Economy & Finance, 2021).

In conclusion, SMR has more favorable qualities than a large nuclear power plant in terms of safety, geographical flexibility, and price. However, SMR is still in the development stage, so there are opinions that question commercialization. In addition, there are issues of radioactive waste including spent nuclear fuel, and since SMR is still a reactor, there is a public opinion to avoid nuclear power plants. Therefore, these problems should be solved through valuable research on SMR. When these problems are solved, SMR will be able to go beyond large nuclear power plants and become a valuable energy source of power generation.

## References

Cho, J. (2023, April 26). Korea-U.S. companies such as Boeing, Exxon Mobil, SK, and Doosan cooperate in SMR, aviation, hydrogen, and robot fields. *The Chosun Ilbo*. https://www.chosun.com/economy/industry-company/2023/04/26/VL4P3Y6M4NGYTEVGKHVCEYFXWU/

Liou, J. (2021, November 4). What are the Small Modular Reactor (SMRs)? *International Atomic Energy Agency*. https://www.iaea.org/newscenter/news/ what-are-small-modular-reactors-smrs

Korea Hydro & Nuclear Power. (2021, April 21). Future Energy Special 2: KHNP's Innovative SMR. *Korea Hydro & Nuclear Power*. https://blog.naver.com/ i_love_khnp/222317527927

Korea Hydro & Nuclear Power. (2021, April 28). Future Energy Special 3: KHNP's Innovative SMR. *Korea Hydro & Nuclear Power*. https://blog.naver.com/ i_love_khnp/222326353842

Ministry of Economy & Finance. (2021, August 25). Re-leap of Nuclear Power Plant with SMR. *Ministry of Economy & Finance*. https://blog.naver.com/mosfnet/ 222483553916

Polaris Market Research. (2022). Small modular reactor market size. *Small Modular Reactor Market Size Global Report, 2022-2030*

PRESENTATION

## 1. Reviewing Your Visual Aids

Look through your visual aids. Use the following questions to check how effective and useful the visual aids are in aiding your presentation.

- Are they attractive and simple?
- Can the audience obtain the main ideas of the presentation from the visuals?
- Are there images or elements that are not explained in the presentation speech?
- Are all images labelled, and citations given where needed?
- Did you include a Citations List on the final slide?
- Are the contents of the visual aids all relevant to the speech you will give?
- Is the information recent and/or appropriate for your points?
- Are fonts, images and general design consistent throughout?
- Can the slides be navigated and understood quickly, or do they require too much audience decoding time?

## 2. Q&A

Question and Answer sessions are a key part of any presentation. Coming at the end of a presentation, they are a chance for the audience to question the presenter on contents from the presentation. They can be the trickiest part of a presentation, but they can also be opportunities to demonstrate to the audience that you are both assured in your contents, and highly knowledgeable about the topic.
Here are six guidelines for dealing with Q&A:

**A. Tell the audience that you will take questions after the presentation.**

It is important that the audience does not interrupt the presenter, especially as presentations have a limited amount of time. You can inform the audience in the introduction that questions will be taken at the end of the presentation.

*"I will take questions after the presentation."*

**B. Acknowledge the person asking the question.**

When an audience member asks a question, it is polite to acknowledge them for asking. In addition, it gives the presenter time to think about the question before giving an answer.

*"That is a very good question…"*
*"Thank you for the question…"*
*"That is a very interesting point…"*

**C. Ask the questioner to repeat it if you do not hear it.**

You might miss a question due to background noise, the questioner's speaking style or volume, or perhaps you just misheard an important part of the question. In these cases, it is best to ask the questioner to repeat the question.

*"I am sorry; could you repeat that for me please?"*
*"I could not quite catch that, could you repeat it one more time please?"*

### D. Ask the questioner to rephrase it if you do not understand it.

There are situations when you may not understand the question at all. In this case, you can ask the audience member to rephrase the question. This should be a cue to change the style used in the question.

> *"I am sorry, could you rephrase that for me please?"*
> *"That is an interesting point, could you rephrase it for the audience please?"*

### E. If you do not know the answer on the spot, do not panic! Inform them that you will get back to them later.

If you simply do not know an answer to a question, do not say 'I don't know,' but say you 'will respond' in greater detail later.'

> *"That is a very important question, but is also a very complicated one. Please leave me your email so that I can get back to you!"*
> *"That requires a long and detailed answer! Please see me after the presentation and let's talk about it."*

### F. Anticipating Questions

A great way to prepare for a Q&A session is to think about what you could be asked. You should make a note of which parts of your argument required the most persuasion, as this is an area where the audience may ask more critical questions. You can also present the content to your peers before the presentation and have them come up with anticipated questions.

## 3. Cue Cards

Cue cards can be very helpful to presenters who are anxious or nervous. They are a useful tool; they can help you present, but more importantly, they are great for helping you practice. You should think of cue cards as part of your presentation preparation. They will help you feel comfortable when practicing and allow you to move away from a strict script and be able to speak more naturally. As you practice, remake your cue cards, but with fewer words each time, until you are comfortable without them. You can always bring cue cards to a presentation and use them when necessary!

### Tips for cue cards

1. Only use key words
2. Number each card and make sure your writing/printing is legible
3. Use as many as you need
4. You can annotate them to help you with gestures and voice
5. Use actual card, not paper!
6. Clip the cards together
7. You do not need to use them, but they can be a good back-up

## 4. Model Presentation Script

### Success of Australia's Tourism

**[Hook]** Have you travelled overseas this year? Is there anyone who has been to Europe? How about Australia? Anyone? Oh, Jenny, you have been to Australia. Which city did you visit? Sydney. Excellent. **[Greeting]** Hello, my name is David, majoring in Tourism. **[Focus statement]** According to Department of Foreign Affairs and Trade, Australia's tourism industry contributes 3.2% to Australia's income. Today, I am going to talk about why Australia's tourism is successful. The reason I chose this topic is because I was captivated by Australia's natural wonders during my recent visit and its booming tourism industry. **[Preview]** So, I am going to focus especially on the breathtaking landscapes, unique wildlife, and its distant location. **[Transition]** Are you ready? Let's begin.

**[Main point 1]** First, I would like to talk about Australia's unique geological and ecological features, which make it a particularly attractive tourist location. According to a survey, close to 70% of tourists said a key reason to go to Australia is its extraordinary natural phenomena. Let's look at some examples of that. The first example is Uluru. It is the world's largest stone. This formation is so rare that the Uluru-Kata Tjuta National Park is one of the few World Heritage properties listed for both its natural and cultural values. Another example is beaches. Australia has over 10,000 miles of white sandy beaches, and some of the world's best surfing conditions, which attract locals and tourists alike. These two examples alone make me feel like I want to go back to Australia and travel around. How about you?

**[Transition]** Now, let's go deeper into the second captivating aspect that attracts numerous tourists from around the world to Australia.

**[Main point 2]** Australia is well-known for the diversity of its wildlife, so nature lovers flock there to catch glimpses of Australia's unique animals, insects, birds and sea creatures. According to this chart from DRET, the Great Barrier Reef particularly ranks as the most popular tourist destination in Australia - have you heard of it? It's an incredible coral ecosystem that is over 2,300 kilometers long! Divers who explore the reef can see beautiful underwater scenery and a diverse array of sea creatures, such as clownfish and sea turtles. Meanwhile, on land, there are a number of animals to be found that are unique to Australia, such as kangaroos, koalas and wombats. These creatures are symbolic of Australia, and the chance to see them in their natural habit is an opportunity that nature lovers should not miss.

**[Transition]** Finally, let's talk about the third reason for Australia's success as a tourist destination – its location.

**[Main point 3]** Australia is physically very distant from the rest of the world. In fact, the average traveler to Australia spends 17 hours on flights just to reach there. That is twice as long as to other major tourist hubs in the world. Is this a problem? Not necessarily! Australia offers many unique places to visit in a single trip and it is also considered a safe place to travel. And despite the distance being a factor in Australia having fewer visitors, those visitors on average spend three times as long visiting the country as they do in most other countries – basically, because it is so much harder to get to Australia, visitors like to stay longer to really make the most of their trip. With a longer trip, visitors to Australia are able to spend time to have a unique and varied travel experience, making the country a premier destination for travelers.

**[Review]** In conclusion, let's recap the key points covered in today's presentation. Australia's attraction lies in its stunning landscapes, distinct wildlife, and its remote location, which adds a sense of adventure and novelty for many travelers.

**[Concluding remarks]** So, the next time you plan your trip, why don't you consider going to Australia? You won't be disappointed! Thank you.

## 5. Research Proposal Presentation Script

### Topic Proposal:
### The Progress and Practical Uses of Synthetic Speech

Think about your typical daily routine. Perhaps you ask Siri a quick question before leaving the house, and then you take the bus or subway and hear the announcements for the stops. Swiping your ID card, a voice confirms that you have opened or locked a door. As the technology around us has developed, it has become more common to hear synthetic voices being used for announcements, information, and even entertainment. Although a significant amount of progress has been made in this field, is there still room for improvement? Or have we already gone too far? Hello, my name is Jisoo Kang and I'm from the computer science department. Today, I'd like to tell you about my proposed topic for this semester; 'The progress of synthetic speech so far.' I'll first of all give you some basic information about my topic, and then I will explain why I chose it. Finally, I'll show you three research sources that I hope will help me to develop this topic more.

Let me start by giving some of the background of this topic. As I said, we often hear synthetic voices in our everyday lives. Most synthetic speech is produced by text-to-speech (TTS) systems – this means, written text is put through the system and a device 'reads' the text out loud. It has various uses. For example, it can be used by those with visual impairments or reading disabilities to hear words that are written on their screen. You might also have tried it when using translation apps, so that you could hear how to pronounce the words or phrases you've checked. As I showed at the start, it's also commonly used on public transport and at stations, announcing the arrival of buses and trains. It's an incredibly useful tool that has been around since the 1980s, and the pace of development has picked up especially in the past decade. But how much further can this development go? In the next part, I'd like to expand on this and explain why I chose my topic.

Many news articles and forums discuss some of the great developments in speech synthesis that can benefit people with speech disorders or impairments. Such tech has been around for a while; Professor Stephen Hawking famously used a Voice Output Communication Aid (VOCA) from the late 1980s until his death. Recently, the focus of research is on making that synthetic speech as natural sounding as possible, or even finding ways to recreate the user's own accent and tone. However, like many recent technological developments, synthetic speech can be a double edged sword. One of the many concerns is that it may be used in cybercrime, such as fraud or blackmail. AI can already be used to recreate the image and voice of a celebrity, for example, but if this technology were to be abused, it could have devastating effects on people's lives. This is something we need to be aware of and ensure that counter-measures detect when such tech is being used. For these reasons, I find this topic to be both interesting and worthy of our attention.

While considering this topic, I found three research sources that I think will help me to trace the progression of synthetic speech. The first is an article by Nicholas Weiler from the University of California San Francisco, about recent research that seeks to generate speech using brain recordings. As mentioned earlier, this is one way that speech synthesis can help those who have lost their voices. Machine learning is a big part of the continued progress of TTS, so my second research source comes from Kim, Kong and Son, whose research includes an end-to-end TTS system that promises to generate more natural sounding audio than what is currently available. This research was conducted in 2021, so it is very recent information. Finally, I found a paper by Wenger et al. from 2021. This paper discusses how speech synthesis can be used in cyber-crimes related to speaker recognition and voice sign-in protocols. It highlights a key issue that may arise as synthetic speech progresses.

I hope that my speech today has given you some insight into my topic for this semester and my reasoning for choosing this topic. Thank you for listening.

## References


Kim, J. H., Kong, J. I., & Son, J. H. (2021). Conditional Variational Autoencoder with Adversarial Learning for End-to-End Text-to-Speech. *Proceedings of the 38th International Conference on Machine Learning*. https://proceedings.mlr.press/v139/kim21f.html

Weiler, N. (2019, April 24). Synthetic Speech Generated from Brain Recordings. *University of California San Francisco* https://www.ucsf.edu/news/2019/04/414296/synthetic-speech-generated-brain-recordings

Wenger, E., Bronckers, M., Cianfarani, C., Cryan, J., Sha, A., Zheng, H., and Zhao, B. Y. (2021). "Hello, It's Me": Deep Learning-based Speech Synthesis Attacks in the Real World. In Proceedings of the 2021 ACM SIGSAC Conference on Computer and Communications Security (CCS '21). *Association for Computing Machinery*, 235–251. https://doi.org/10.1145/3460120.3484742

WRITERS

**Hye-Jin Hawkes**
**Michael Brandon**
**Hugh Newton**
**Kimberley Blount**

EDITORS

**Yuah V. Chon**
**Kyungsook Kim**
**Hye-Jin Hawkes**

REVIEWERS

**Yuah V. Chon**
**Kyungsook Kim**
**Hye-Jin Hawkes**
**Connie Park**

---

### Hye-Jin Hawkes

Associate Professor at Hanyang University
PhD. & BSc (Hons) in Biotechnology
Graduate Certificate in Higher Education
Has published 20 academic and business books and translated 2 books
Has published peer-reviewed articles on redox, antioxidant and fermentation in biotechnology

### Michael Brandon

Associate Professor at Hanyang University
MA (Res) & BA (Hons) in History, Geography & International Development. MEd in TESOL
Doctoral Candidate in International Education Administration
Has published peer-reviewed articles on second language curriculum and educational technology

### Hugh Newton

Associate Professor at Hanyang University
BA in English Literature & B.Comm (Hons) in Creative Writing
MA in TESOL
Has published two collections of short stories, two graphic novels and edited three children's books

### Kimberley Blount

Associate Professor at Hanyang University
BSc (Combined Hons) in Politics and Sociology
MA in TESOL
Cambridge DELTA
Experience teaching Business English in three countries, as well as Academic English and IELTS preparation

### Yuah V. Chon

Professor at Hanyang University, Department of English Education
PhD. in English Language Teaching & MA in TESL
Has published peer-reviewed articles on second language writing and technology-assisted language learning
Teaches courses in materials evaluation and development at undergraduate and graduate levels

### Kyungsook Kim

Senior researcher for the College English Education Center at Hanyang University
PhD in English Language Teaching & MA in TEFL
Has published peer-reviewed articles on connection between reading and writing, second language writing, vocabulary teaching, and English for specific purpose (ESP)

### Connie Park

Assistant Professor at Hanyang University
MS Ed. In TESOL & BA in English Language and Literature
Acknowledged for the contribution in the book publication of How to Teach Business English, Pearson Longman
Has extensive experience teaching Business English at Samsung, and other corporations, as well as English Language, Theory, and Methodology at universities

# ACADEMIC HORIZONS:
## Skills Across Disciplines

한양대학교 대학영어교육위원회 편

**펴낸날** 2024년 1월 30일 초판 1쇄

**펴낸이** 이기정 ● **펴낸곳** 한양대학교 출판부 ● **출판등록** 제4-7호(1972.2.29)

**주소** 서울 성동구 왕십리로 222 ● **전화** 02.2220.1432-4 ● **팩스** 02.2220.1435

**홈페이지** press.hanyang.ac.kr ● **이메일** presshy@hanyang.ac.kr

**표지** 안광일 ● **본문디자인·편집** 김민지 ● **인쇄** 네오프린텍



값 20,000 원

**ISBN** 978.89.7218.799.8 (93740)